THE
WONDER LAND
OF LOVE

Books
By Agene Justice Onotiemoria

AVAILABLE FROM APMI PUBLICATIONS,
AMAZON.COM AND OTHER RETAIL OUTLETS

LOVE DISTINGUISHED - SERIES TWO

THE WONDER LAND OF LOVE

AGENE JUSTICE ONOTIEMORIA

Book 2 of a 5 Book Series
Love Distinguished

BOOK TITLE: **The Wonderland of Love**
Book Series, Love Distinguished 2 of 5

WRITTEN BY AGENE JUSTICE ONOTIEMORIA
Paperback ISBN: 978-1-909132-30-6
eBook ISBN: 978-1-909132-83-2

Published By:
APMI Publications
In Partnership with Truth for the Journey Books
Email: publications@alanpateman.com
www.AlanPatemanMinistries.com

Acknowledgements:
Cover Design Copyright APMI
Senior Editor/Publisher: Dr. Alan Pateman
Editing/Proofreading/Research: Dr. Jennifer Pateman
Computer Administration/Office Manager: Dr. Dorothea Struhlik
Cover Image Credit: www.PosterMyWall.com

Unless otherwise indicated, all scriptural quotations are from the King James Version of the bible.

*Where scriptures appear with special emphasis (**in bold,** italic or <u>underlined</u>) we have edited them ourselves in order to bring focused attention within the context of this subject being taught.*

Dedication

I dedicate this book to my unquestionable God, who saw me as a worthy fountain pen to reach the world. I dedicate it to my biological brothers and sisters, both at home and abroad, including my parents who always keep up with their support, you are my backbone. In addition my mentors and benefactors, well done, let's work together as a team for solid achievement. I also dedicate this work to all of my well-wishers, pastors, brethren and friends, whether home or abroad your "Hi," means a lot to me. Keep it up. God bless you all.

Table of Contents

Acknowledgement

I would like to take this opportunity to acknowledge Dr Alan Pateman and his wonderful team at Alan Pateman Ministries International, for all of their hard work and dedication in: revising, proofreading, editing, and doing all of the important preparations required, in order to present a book like this for publication. Including the cover and art work etc.

I am appreciative for Dr Alan's foresight in all the above. And this includes making this book, The Wonderland of Love *(as well as the other 4 books in this series entitled "Love Distinguished")*, readily available on international outlets such as Amazon, iBookStore, Nook Store, Kobo Store, Walmart, Bol, Rakute, Google, Allegro, and other big platforms, as an eBook as well as a paperback. What an opportunity to get the word out!

Foreword

For many years I have been studying this subject of love, as displayed in human nature, also within the bible. Love has many facets and manifestations and it is my intention that through this series, Love Distinguished, *(this is book 2 of 5)* we will look at the biblical definition of love, including its many other expressions—within society and life in general. We will look at love, in both its negative and positive expressions—appropriate and inappropriate—yet far too many to list here.

From my Nigerian background, it has been said that I have a typically straight forward, no nonsense talking style! But also a unique viewpoint from which we can be open together and discuss many random and even uncomfortable topics; allowing God to bring us to the right conclusions about this immensely vast topic.

Introduction

I can see many hearts bleeding, even though their cheeks pump for laughter, which shine like a reflection of happiness yet they're still very dull deep down. They try to conceal their sorrow and tears, yet their minds seem to continually fuel their pain. They are like those who receive punches without and have no tears to confirm their pain. There's no sign to express their pains or feelings because they lack real contact with the right people.

No matter how much they try and express themselves to others, they find no one with equal experiences. Plus it's so very difficult to learn from the mistakes of others.

Abused Love

Some like to say, *"Confidence is the weapon for killing problems,"* and always give the appearance that they are so very bold, strong and healthy, yet something is still missing. And they might dress with decency, maybe for attention— even like a queen or king—yet feel like a servant inside. Only they are aware of this perhaps, until one day their grief gets out of control and all those around them begin to call them angry and frustrated.

How are you? To some perhaps you appear okay, while to others, there is just nothing good about you; but only you know that you can't just help your abused love. You are like a wounded lion; one that only the Lord God including the delegated bodies can understand. Some laugh at you whenever they see you. While others gloat that you are in pain; at least you are not better than them. What a world!

You know what it is like to express love in action emotionally, physically, financially and in support and yet it is turned down by whom you tend to love. You could really be the one who does not count on race, colour, education, social class, grades, family and wealth, but regardless of all your efforts to build up a true love for a relationship, it is being totally turned against you.

Broken

O! You have been over broken, to the extent there is nothing anybody can do to break you because what he or she tends to break has a million times been broken into pieces already. You have been immune and recovered from the shock and pain. None are aware of this. Some mockers tend to use their strategies to charge your sorrow and bitterness. Behold, they have not the appropriate insight to see that you have graduated, (you are in your workshop of destiny) whereby the lessons thereof are meant for you alone, which you have learnt already and that you now know how to control your sorrow and bitterness (Isa. 30:20-21).

Hence, their expected negative report about you are nothing but a total failure and a disappointment to them. Little did they know that you no longer cry as usual but now learn how to restrain yourself; shame on them that you have gotten your lullaby. You are conscious of how the evil arrows come to manipulate you for their glory. No weapon fashioned against you shall prosper (Isa. 54:17).

And you are aware of what it takes to be close to a fellow and yet not confide in them, even fear him. You have over trusted people and failed severely to the point that you no longer trust anybody. Why? Because past pain lingers long and remains fresh in your mind, it only takes the grace of God for someone that has had that kind of experience to forget overnight just like that.

Truth Never Dies

In short, it's like whatever happens to a child, it stays long in their minds and grows with them. You try, but you just can't help to put the memory behind you. Your human efforts are not enough. Your mind keeps whispering to you that you start thinking that the present fellow is just the same as the former, with all assumptions. And so, you prefer to close it up and resign to resentment, as a calculation to quenching the fire of failure and disappointment.

You know that truth has no friends. Truth is humanly regarded alone, but because God is involved it can never die. And that is even why truth is dangerous with unquenchable light of which both of them are original. If your styles are truthfulness and honesty, even integrity, believe you me, you are alone and on your own, because someone somewhere somehow has seen you and has viewed you a complete disadvantage. *"A fly can never support anyone without a sore."*

Hence, following you is totally futile, based on their motives. Conclusively they have already written you off — even if you dance acrobatics until tomorrow! The bible says, *"Can two work together except they are of the same spirit"* (Amos 3:3). Secondly, the bible also says, *"who can understand the heart of man, it is desperately wicked, full of deceit and evil"* (Jer. 17:9-10). Attention please, no born element is completely free, except God grants it. *"Whosoever the son of man free is free indeed"* (John 8:36).

Inexperienced elements expect you to deal with a broken relationship or marriage so easily. However hard you try to make them understand that it is not as simple as they thought, they ever remain far from the truth because you have been cut too deep. They are just so far behind your mind-set and motive, even thoughts and memories. Your points of view are different things altogether. They just don't have the eyes to see — that you have been left with sores — that take a longer time to heal.

Limit yourself from being Continually Victimised

Even as you are trying to take a deep breath, there comes another fellow who is ready to cause you some disasters, much more than what the previous had done. There are agents specifically delegated on the errand of worsening your situation. They can appear with a claim and all humilities, as a solution to your problem. Therefore, if you realise that it is a common experience with humans in life, you learn to apply wisdom in your contact and dealings with others, in order to limit yourself from being continually victimised. A man is half positive and half negative. One time mister Peter can be very good to you, while another time he can be so very bad. The root is from the garden of Eden. Be informed that the issues of life bring experience but you still need people and they still need you.

However your next steps should pursue a solution, such that can uplift your spirit as a result of your hard experiences of a shattered love. There is no harm in trying. It is a matter of life. There is no escape in anything pertaining to life in general. I would advise hence, one should endure one's experience, as problems are not forever and with time adversities subside. Do stop being a single, but think of how to be two in one.

Problem Solving

See, we have been discussing casting blame on each of the opposite sex, I mean lady against guy and guy against lady, as if that is the solution. Look! If you don't solve what poses as a problem to you, it will keep recurring and do you know what that means? Repeating the same mistakes. A test or trial of our faith makes many repeat their human classes of life several times. It is not by size, muscle, height, or the wisdom of man, rather by maturity with divine help. *"By strength shall no man prevail"* (1 Sam. 2:9).

If you don't deal with your situation, it will always be there, waiting for you, (such as your landlord!) Attention please, I put it on us that half of our problems are a result of our mistakes, due to ignorance. So, it is high time you started dealing with your case before a good Samaritan comes in to help you out. If I should pinpoint some of them right now, you find out that you and I are not left out of the blame. Starting from manners (like being lippy), which robs the mind of happiness and joy. Some people with wrong laughter (mockery) can make others cry, so if you are that type of person, you need to change. It is not helping any issue for good around you.

The Realm of Emotional Lust

By the way, why do you prefer another, to the one you have? Even when strolling together, you don't even mind expressing your feelings openly, by spying at the opposite sex. Actions speak louder than words. In conversations, you can only voice out what you have inside of you. I can judge such feelings, if I am permitted. I can put it on you that such a glance with uncontrollable expressions and feelings are deeply rooted in the realm of emotional lust. It is what you think inside of you that births such lustfulness.

In the deliverance ministry, demons are usually responsible for the fuelling of emotional lust, which birth sexual perversions. And may the good Lord help us in this trend in Jesus' name. If you can't completely take your eyes off of any woman, it is not 100% your fault because powers are responsible in some areas of your life. Pray to God for help (Matt. 10:36; Ps. 91:15-16).

If Christ Tarries

And in that case, do not expect the other to think that he or she is still in your priority? O! Spare me of that your total fallacy. In the real sense, if you feel so very superior over your date, why did you condescend to date the one who is so inferior to yourself? And by the way, who is not important? No matter who you are, you can't say you're not human?

Can you consume another nature different from what God has naturally given to everybody to consume, such as: air, rain, due, sun and moon without a demand of payment? Of course not, then please, try and control the natural ego that we all are given by our Creator. Nobody is an animal. We all met the world like this and certainly we're all going to leave it in like manner, if Christ tarries.

Chapter 1

Fake and Genuine Love

False Humility

So much fake is love that people claim to practice or exercise towards one another. You can hardly rebuke and turn away anybody who fakes humility by coming to you in the name of a fake love, claiming that he or she is interested in you. You can hardly even understand such a one under this shadow except with spiritual insight. You can never doubt a fake love if you are watchful with the eyes of God.

Do you have spiritual insight or the spirit of discernment? You can beat many problems by faith because you have a basic understanding. When you critically analyse a fake love, it will tell you that it ends is dissimulation. Tracing it back to the foundation, you find out that it was because of material and financial acquisition or one or two other reasons that made him or her come around you for a love.

What you have gathered in most cases is what some fellows actually used in respecting and accepting you closer not really that you have worth as an individual to their naked eyes. Do you have clothes? You therefore have worth owing to that. Or are you the type that always dresses with correct and fine outfits elegantly? You have worth without a second thought. You will get to know and sense it from the breath and love of others; while you are carefully walking across the street.

The Fake Lover

A fake lover will say if you don't sell drugs and live like every other drug addict, you are not his or her desirable friend or a worthy personality to identify with. If care is not taken you might be a mistake friend as regarded inwardly by the very person in question. Or in a similar case, if you are not a business person consider your relationship with him or her a forgotten issue.

Some groups of fake elements only like yellow persons and the purely white people for friends because of beauty. While other personalities to them are complete gorillas by colours. That is the reason you see people bleaching just to be able to gain acceptance or even match with the required colour to be favoured by, witches, demons, occult powers, humans and others who are really concerned about that. May the good living God help us in Jesus' name.

A Holy Dress Code

Many are single lover — ladies who prefer guys that are completely orphans: no father, no mother, and if possible the only sons of their parents. If you are living alone, that is when they listen to you at all. Or better still, you have immediate cash at hand to offer. Some gangster loving ladies will say, *"Why don't you start plaiting your hair and start wearing earrings in your ears?"*

Ask me for what purpose would a man begin putting on women's materials or attires, just to woo the love of a woman to himself or to be loved by her? The only people that the Lord God specifically recommended and allowed to wear rope were the priests. They were marked with an outstanding mode of dress, which enabled them to carry a kind of identification different from every other person (Levities/priests) just for their special ministry in the temple of God (Ex. 28:2).

They used it to minister in the holy of holies before (B.C.) the era of Jesus Christ (salvation). And every other person tempts God if attempted. It is forbidden and it can attract punishment even with death. It is a total madness to do that as a rational fellow.

We know that today, the global cultural systems have changed and many are actually dancing to it. She may give reasons why she prefers guys like that for a love. Some will not even want you to keep company with friends the moment they step into your life. Indirectly, she is telling you all your casual friends and others should be driven away. If you are the type who love party or not, they would want to know. They will also prefer you have the interest in taking them to restaurants to eat almost every evening. Some ladies also prefer indoor guys while others would want the types who are always outdoors.

There may be spiritual reasons behind the latter. In the sense, she may not always want the man around when the powers or the beast would come to visit her for their usual contact. She might not be comfortable with the presence of the man while their usual business is going on. That is if she is the type who always wants the man out without accompanying him out. At times, they would want to make a stroll for some window shopping during which it may necessitate them to sit in a relax-able post and gist all days.

The Genuine Lover

A genuine lover is very calculative in his or her dealings with the neighbours or friends. He or she can never pose any stress on you. He or she is very much aware for example, that too much phone calling is a complete disturbance and a thought provoking issue. This is because each day has its day-today activities by man in search for bread. And that there is time for everything which happens under the sun (Eccles. 3:1).

And that imposes unnecessary responsibility on someone who claims that to love is a considerable kind of act, to rival with one's project and responsibilities.

If a turbulent blockage — caused by non-living things — is ten per cent, then the remaining ninety per cent must be caused by living things, in form of animals, plants, grasses, fishes, birds, including human beings as the worst of all. There is no genuine lover who would fail to support the other physically, emotionally and in prayer to succeed.

Are all those compulsory as a yardstick to measure a true love? Absolutely no. Genuine love considers godly motives and righteousness. Provided both of you love each other with a true love, because two good heads are better than one. Every other thing must come as an addition to them (Matt. 6:33).

CHAPTER 2

Ironic Love

Actions Speaks Louder than Words

This is a situation whereby some elements deliberately insist on the opposite side of an issue, that they know what they are doing only to discover at last that reverse is the case altogether. When you really take time to find out and watch what they are doing, it somehow reflects that their way is cunning and trickish to the whole issue. It does happen in relationships and in business circles generally.

Sometimes, when you are (or not) together, they mean something else for real. There could be some indirect enemies who may be so very close to you that you would be thinking they are your best friends. But thanks be to the Lord for His gift of wisdom and for the wise ones who quickly realise that when you make friends, you must not be too hasty to trust and rely on them. A mirage can be dangerous sometimes and some so called friends are very good in tricking and obtaining from you, through many processes. If you critically analyse their motives, it is typically baseless, in the sense that they are just looking for an opportunity to be laughing at you.

A Traitor has Emerged

Imagine, a fellow running helter-skelter in search for a place to lay his head; at this process tears nearly rush down his cheeks. Behold, having been favoured by you, he would want to claim ownership of you, both physically and spiritually. If you are a good person with a good heart, if you offered anything to someone you are in trouble and if you accept offers from anybody you are also in trouble.

Your subjects automatically become his or her subjects of the day. He or she will want to fully claim everything you have overnight. Why? Human beings, where are we going? The irony of love, and if care is not taken you who were living peacefully in your house before, will begin to experience a nightmare with unnecessary interferences, and with your joy being shattered.

You wanted to come to his or her level, just being considerate for integration, but instead your goodness and generosity are now being used against you. Within your house a traitor has emerged. Let me say that anybody who causes an innocent fellow division in his or her own home, is a complete traitor and a witch to the core, even a devil incarnate.

An Imposter

Imagine, your neighbour assuming the position of an unpaid contractor (rumour monger) in your house. Whatever you eat, public people must know of it. I'm not referring to spouses or children, brothers, sisters, parents, or relatives, rather an incomplete head of tuber of a yam giving you a headache in your own house, for just no genuine reason. A nobody. An imposter. An image from the blue! May God help us. Is it not really a true saying that your food to your enemies is like a bullet in their gun to gun you down. May our good God deliver us and judge them.

Job was an example on this basis. It happened that those he fed, later turned around to spy on him with a claim to be checking on him, with bad motives concealed up in their minds; wanting just to know how bad his situation really was! Even in his presence, they weren't ashamed with old memories in their skulls. Guess what? They were spitting even before his naked eyes, as a way of telling him, *"Look guy you are smelling, phew!"* This was Job who used to feed them and flex them with his money (Job 30:9-10).

Whom have you organised a banquet to feed? I dare you to find out that amongst them there is a Judah (not to praise God) but a fake type of Judah who is seeking your downfall. But don't forget the God of simplicity Who protects the simple and will deal with them in order to protect you (Ps. 116:6).

A nobody from unknown where! Why? Not that it's bad to favour or render help to anybody, it's just that we all in the group have not taken time to find out the solution to the problems against any act of generosity. For example, watch people with good hearts, their problem is that they feel and conclude that everyone is like them.

Indoor Rats are a Menace!

Why is it that people are choosing just to be wicked against their innocent neighbour? It is a witchcraft practice somehow and somebody would need a genuine repentance. An indoor rat is never tired of relating every current info about you to menace. Please, info disseminates change from your wickedness for good; for evil does no longer pay. Look behind and ahead of you traitors. Your problem is as big as mount Ararat, yet you are busy with another man's.

Isn't that funny? Bearing an elephant on your head yet busy excavating a common cricket with your toad, my friend, that is stupidity and in short even a complete foolishness. Do not broadcast (through mockery) about anybody to another fellow, especially if he or she has not wronged you. It is a sort of loading the supposed personality with bitterness. Common laughing at someone, can cut even more than a razor-blade.

May God help someone to juxtapose his or her actions when dealing with their fellow human beings, as not to birth any kind of hurt in them, in all ramifications, in Jesus' name.

Porosity is a Form of Betrayal

Don't even bother to listen if you cannot keep a secrete. Porosity is equivalent to any act of gossip. Betrayers change, as your reward is waiting for you in the prospect. And don't think you can manipulate to escape it. It is not a human tax whereby you can use the influence of a brother or a sister in order to evade it.

Another which is common amongst the human race is that most people love you simply because of what you have to offer them, rather than for loving you as a person. They are cunning personalities. If you have a good heart, you will get to understand that they are very easy to beat and defeat in the name of Jesus, with the gravities in which they operate. The moment their target is exhausted, they dash into thin-air like moth eaten clothes and that is the end. I pray for somebody, may you never be victimised in Jesus' name. Don't be afraid of your fellow humans who come against you in the name of the devil.

Babies are not Trusted with Dangerous Truth

David was not afraid of Goliath. In the human kingdom, such is bound to happen as a way to teaching you a lesson to be wise that life is two or even more. As our parents didn't tell us the truth, we have to learn through pains and by experiences with all drastic curriculum. God sometimes does the same thing (Isa. 30:20-21). And I often hear most of us blame our parents for that. They forget one thing: babyhood. Babies are not trusted with dangerous truth otherwise, our parents would tell us everything. It is quite a pity that we all are immature.

Let me remind you of a secrete; on many occasions your parents attempted to tell you something special but nay pause with a glance at you. Many of us have experienced that on several occasions, on stepping into our sitting rooms—before even taking our seats—our parents have taken a second glance at us, with a lot of unspeakable lies in that look, to the core.

Sometimes when we're honest, actually, we discover that we were all based on what we knew. You can't operate with a degree if you are not a graduate. If you can't write your name, what are you doing with a biro on your hand? Or are you kidding? May the good Lord help us to know where we actually belong. How can you be a tomato seller and you're dragging an office off to the governor of a state. Maybe you going there to ravage and then put the state in more problems.

Reality Check

You were that same person someone wouldn't want to stay, without setting his or her eyes on, how come he now suddenly changed and wouldn't want to set the same eyes on you again? The simple fact is that, you never took any time to really check as to, *"What exactly does this fellow want from me?"* Is it that I am too handsome or rather too beautiful? What makes them particular about me? Am I too much? But little did you know that what makes someone like a bucket is nothing other than its contents; the liquid it carries. The moment the water is finished, it is dumped around the corner.

Being Selective doesn't make you Racist

A mosquito can never stay with you after filling its tank—its belly—with your blood. Wise up somebody for life and dealings have lanes. The fact that *"the sky is broad"* doesn't mean *"a bird should fly haphazardly as broad as the sky,"* rather it must fly on a routine basis. Selecting those that must come around you doesn't make you a racist. Critically analysed, one would find out that there is a reason to every action, as well as reaction. Who just could not do without you before, now can stay away for months without even checking on you or bothering to make a common phone call.

It is a pity. *"My people are dying without knowledge"* the bible says (Hos. 4:6). Consider yourself without a prophetic whispering that you are an enemy now if you were a friend then.

An adage says: *"Don't be surprised when old friends have suddenly turned new enemies."* You didn't check those who were flocking around you during your good times; that is why. As it also turned the other side of the coin, you still didn't get the message cleared. Stop being ignorant every time and then falling victim.

No one seems to talk good about you again because you are no longer that chief, rich and generous person he or she used to know. They have all despised you because, their formal love for you was merely what you gathered, what you had to offer and that you were really helping to the core. None of them who wasn't receiving gifts each from you but continually maintaining a formal relationship with you may reduce their wallet now, because, definitely, they must shoulder one or two responsibilities from you; inasmuch as you are yet to be able to help yourself now. See (Job 30:9-10).

If you manage to run across them again along the way and peradventure they gesticulate you of something because they just don't have any means to dodge you, I bet you their inner man is reading, *"Oh guy, who do you want to induce with additional responsibility with your latest poverty. To hell with you and your bad luck." "This is a bad market today. I didn't know I was supposed to meet you on the way."* May the good God forgive someone.

If you truly hear of sad stories told about generosities being abused, you will have some tears rush down your chicks even though you are not the direct victim. They have no idea of how they should completely avoid you.

Screen their Motives

If any fellow claims to be interested in you or having any kind of love for you, please, take time to scan and screen the motive behind their declaration even before you admit to believe and fully dedicate yourself and be committed to the relationship; I advice you to watch. If you yield in without check, your result might just be negative. We pray it won't be our portion in Jesus' name.

Many have cried who concluded a trust over their so called best of friends—out of ignorance—who ironically fell victim at the last. *"Before even you lied to me"* they say with tears on their faces, *"things have already fallen apart."* I want to say sorry on behalf of all the incompetent fools that do not know the value of a coin. I mean the abused to any good being done to them. Sorry, I know how you feel as an experience person.

But to balance the equation of generosity, I must do justice to both sides that I also blame you that you suppose to look before you leap. The fact that you can help someone out of his or her problem doesn't mean you should just begin to help everybody you see in problem. As a benefactor, everybody is not your beneficiary, take note.

CHAPTER 3

Self/Selfish Love

Lovers of Themselves

Everyone is not the same. Some people love only themselves. Some see others as a nobody even an animal in the open field. Don't be surprised that your so called bosom friend is calling you a monkey in their mind. The impression he or she got of you is so bad such that when unveiled to you, one will be so ashamed because of the doses.

Those you flex up occasionally, don't be surprised your name is a mug by them. This contextual statement could embrace a lot of illustrations that one may not even know. Watch, as we proceed, we shall begin to treat them bit by bit.

These lovers of themselves are of different types. Different types in the sense on the part of homosexuality and lesbianism it is plainly notified. Imagine a feeling of a situation whereby a particular individual will not bother to pay interest to the opposite sex, rather carefully do it all alone: self feelings. And this is carefully carried out by whatsoever materials such as: soap which could be liquid or solid and other related materials. Some use creams to soften it provided they are able to ejaculate/climax. Even animals do not do that. So there is an element—created by the most high God Himself—who now condescend into fooling and stupefying themselves.

Demonic Power

One would begin to question why. You just can't question why. To every decision and even action, there must be a reason behind it, when disclosed you will never nail the person 100% to the cross. Demonic power is fooling people here so much that many are still far behind the truth. Why are human beings victims to this? Second life is a mistake to every born element believe it or not. If a demon works on your privates spiritually, it is only the grace of God that will save you not to sleep with your same blood, even your mother. Many have mated with their fathers, like Lot's daughters for example. Majorities are still doing it till tomorrow.

Can you now blame the victims 100%, absolutely not. If you do you are a devil. Instead, such people need deliverance from God through Jesus Christ our Lord. If you are spiritually inclined by God, you will always be considerate in your dealings with your fellow human beings in any position higher than the person.

A lot is happening in human society. After all, human life is two or even more. It takes a deeper deliverance analysis to deliver and free such a fellow from the real sources of his or her problem in the name of Jesus. That is nature for you. You don't study in a class you don't belong. Do you? In religion, the body of Christ as believers do believe that you must love your neighbour as yourself even if possible much more than yourself. As that is the rule according to the bible. And so, in that case, if such people are found in the midst of Christian believers, they could be a tad self-righteous or fault-finders. In materials, their own is the best.

The spirit of Haughtiness

In schools, they are the best students with adequate wisdom and knowledge. But results tell at the end of the day. Such people do resist positive issues anytime and anywhere. They are very proud to advertise whatever they have. They just can't see far in order to know that life does not entail a competition. They do everything with pride and eye-service even with the spirit of haughtiness. They even strategize to intimidate their neighbours with their possessions. Mostly, the ladies in it, you see every time they demonstrate some swag, then you know a different fellow who is not a member of their group, is in their midst.

In dealings, they are partial with all preferential treatment as the order of their days. They are very discriminative and sentimental. So, almost everything they do is full of selfishness. However you try to move close to them, your intimacy cannot really cut to the base of a relationship with them to any level of satisfaction. But sometimes, when they themselves have a misunderstanding, you do hear their secretes too. From there people get to know that the group is just nothing but making efforts in such a away that the public can feel them. Not really that they are too much.

You are not God as to expect a kind of worship by men. My brother, if you are original you are original, not dubious and nothing can change that. This is to inform somebody that whatever you form yourself to be, which you are naturally and originally not, at the long run must reduce your personality. Therefore, it is advisable that one should maintain one's shoes; otherwise be expecting to be just as clothes do fade away.

Slow and Steady Wins the Race

Apart from the points above, uncontrollable self love can make one become even too speedy in life. And issues of a genuine life do not require any act of competition. Many who have engaged, can really tell all about their sad stories, how they ended up missing so much opportunities. God will help somebody. If you are that type with a long nose, please, try and calm down and reduce a bit of your ego. *"Slow and steady wins the race."* Provided you know yourself and what you actually want (including prayer with faith), God will never fail you, no never, I can assure you. The expectation of the righteous can never be cut off (Prov. 23:18).

I tell you it has cost many their marriages, business connections, even made some unemployed. The highest character anyone can exercise against the other is to look at a fellow human being as an animal. Maids and mistress, servants and masters, employers and employees, business partners, co-workers, colleagues in the office, fellow kings and queens, students and teachers, landlords and tenants, neighbours in the building, brothers and sisters, fellow leaders and many more are all left with percentages on the basis of acceptance to question to order.

Running Helter-Skelter

It has made many to incur problems such that they are even running helter-skelter. If you tell them it is their pride and nothing more, they won't believe it. The seed of a syndrome had been sown in us by demonic powers in order to change our characters for bad, so that we all go about fooling ourselves. We need deliverance in one way or the other. Our behaviour to the Sovereign Lord can also change our characters into stupefying ourselves (Prov. 8:36).

My brother, the glory is on the legs. We are not telling you to be stupid so that humility can be accomplished, not at all. Just to be your simple original self to the glory of God, as you were made. Please, take to be wise. I am not left out, but may the Lord God help all of us and our humanities in Jesus' name in this school of discipline from Jesus' Holy Civilization.

CHAPTER 4

Boyfriend Love

The Demonic School of Thought

Many girls are good and sharp in practising this kind of relationship. This is actually where they exhibit the tactics acquired from the demonic school of thought, from the dark world. They trick and skin men alive here. A single lady will stoop so very low that a bad guy by nick-name who thought he has all the methods it takes to trick any lady, would lose out, ironically concluding that, *"This is the cheap type, I have gotten her already,"* he would say, not knowing she was particular about his virtues.

The moment she got the advantage on her side, she would then show him her real colours and what she was up to in the first place and why she came into his life. At last, the guy bragging just now will only see and hear, *"Look! You are a prey in my hand. You are even a chicken in my pot of soup. Choose what you want now before I do anything silly here."*

Look before you Leap

Even though a single lady could look an empty keg into fetching water, before your naked eyes, be careful. The legs of a single lady can never open without a target, believe it or not. Even some married women are under the control of demonic influences on this basis with their husbands against their affairs.

They are so very sharp that they could have up to about four to five boys/girlfriends at the same time. They do it with different phones, different numbers, different characters, different lifestyles; different modes of dress and manner of approaching everything differently, from A to Z. So, when they are with A they know that they are with A and the same thing with B to Z. If you are not vigilant or spiritual, you can never catch them red handed. You can imagine how the secretes of such a fellow would be. Some ladies mate as many guys or men as possible and yet go for lesbianism.

They categorise their dates based on feelings and capability regards action and in cares; including handsomeness. They know the attachment and the honest ignorance of men. They could even store their phone numbers as: *"Mug one"* or *"Monkey two"* as the case may be. Can I hear somebody say, *"Phew, I feel like vomiting."* No, it shouldn't irritate you towards any kind of vomit; rather it is the drastic experience of our sick human society, where some bad fellows are concerned.

Mostly when they have some of their so called boyfriends or girlfriends around, they will so polish their doings to try to look extra good in their outfits, in order to be seen by their friends. The fact that they are able to do this is none other than they have many suppliers. Similarly, they also have some of the boys they put in wheelchairs. A wheelchair in the sense that they are like a remote control in their hands, for a business. They trade physically and spiritually on their heads.

Robbing Peter to Pay Paul

Any lady who has this mentality on her head, rates men by grades — in kinds and in cash — including physical fitness. If he is a handsome-guy, even though he doesn't have the physical cash to offer yet, she just wouldn't mind taping resources by going the extra mile to extort money from other random guys, in order to support him for dating her. Can you imagine such a perversion. What a decaying impact! Robbing Peter to pay Paul.

She could decide to make others chase her like a sport. How? She already knows that the rest are not in her capital agenda. They are nothing but a pay-loader to her. By reluctantly answering their calls and visiting them occasionally, it's a complete whisper to message them. She is very sharp in constructing stories, as taxing some of them every now and then.

The reverse can also become the case in the sense, the particular one who sees the real her may not be that economically productive but because in action, he is a professional, you see her succumbing to his instructions and orders. It is only when she is confused in creating distinctions that she seeks advice from the girlfriends. This is possible, when the guys are doing eventually the same thing.

Too Many Cooks can Spoil the Broth

You know sometimes too many cooks can spoil the soup but my suggestion is why not stick to a particular kind of style of cooking your meal? Remember, there still existing an adage which says: *"He who chases two rats at once will likely miss both."*

Another stage or level is qualifications. Education is enough for a lady to make her choice, as though she would eat glory. Having not arrived at her final state of prerequisite in making her choices, this time around, she is relatively tired of running to and fro or here and there. So, all she can do is resign herself to staying with him — fairly and squarely — recognising that no choice is ever perfect enough. Therefore in the end, no one eats glory. (Job is another very good example, which is important).

A stable and steady reliable income is necessary as an additional reason in support for a choice of a life partner; otherwise, one could die in hunger. The fact that you are carefully, selectively and systematically arranging your choices shouldn't be judged wrongly, as there's always a reason that onlookers don't know about. Some could go as far as the length as investigating the family background of the man in question, as to whether he has any criminal record or not.

Including whether he or any of his family members had ever been accused of witchcraft, (attacking people using witchcraft practices, diabolical powers or charms etc.), which is something that she'd need to know about. Some could even have other wives and thereby conceal this fact in order to deceive another into becoming another wife or date.

In a similar case he may have even been on a relationship and yet looking for another as though he is looking for a customer. No responsible woman likes sharing her man or husband with another woman. And you can see here that the one who is not faithful is now looking for a faithful personality to date; either way she must know within her own mind before hand. May God help mankind, especially those who use such trickery and deceit.

However, let us not go too far here and discourage people who have an interest in marriage. This book has been written to help you resolve different situations and questions, which need answering from a reliable source. If one has secretly met with one's solution over one's problem, then there's no need to involve an irrelevant third party who might be lapsing.

She may be unfortunate to have her boat of targeted personality capsize to the other side of the lake on her: disappointment due to her being cheated on by the guy during her relationship, because he didn't expect he was going to be her future husband. And that she may end up only to discover that the formally rejected one, during her date is now even ready for a husband. No doubt, she must be ashamed to identify.

Handsomeness and financial measures may disappoint her because already made started from somewhere you did not know. Her targeted guy in question has equally met with people too. Probably, he might be concealing up something all this while; which may later come to her notice. Information on her absence may have the relationship turn the other side of the coin. And so yet again, whoever chases two rats may be unlucky to have none of them at the end of the day. If you find one concentrate on that; this option will definitely satisfy you.

Many girls have allowed bad men or guys to lecture them on how to trick to collect money from their dates, in order to wreck them and all that. But the good ones will never apply such advice into their choice of home to be. Consequently, many bad ladies have equally incurred a figure-head in their matrimonial home, if at all they were lucky enough to settle down. We all know already whatsoever a man sows that he or she must reap. If you manoeuvre to have a child via kidnapers (who stole from others to give you) in order to bail you out from the shame of not being able to have your own.

Be prepared someday you might just be threatened to have your secrete disclosed and you might be required to pay a huge ransom. In that case, you are forced to impose on your husband undue expenses. And that you must agree with me will be a minus for his wallet. But if you carry your fake pregnancy into your matrimonial home, you might expect that some day.

May the good Lord deliver us. The world system in the hand of man is a complete imperfect system. It is completely under demonic control and influence.

Chapter 5

Girlfriend Love

There's an Expiry Date

So many guys are very good in dating more than just one girl at a time. This issue cannot be over emphasised. How? If you don't have more than one tongue, you just can't do it. Majority of this set of people are so desperate in that if they want a particular girl, they just don't mind spending heaven and earth, in order to have her. They can even go extra miles as applying diabolical powers and charms in order to get her. There could arouse a contemplation such that along the line complications could set in to result impossibility, but with the help of charms, assurance is possible. To that, take note there is an expiry date.

Worse of all, a bad woman can spoil another woman, they could spend even through her friend provided she fall to her expected mood by the guy in question. One would begin to imagine what is in a single lady that someone would go that far in search for her?

The content in her is what makes negative people be particular about her. A situation whereby a lady is spiritually endowed with a certain amount of wealth and who wasn't present but spiritually inclined from that perspective of the kingdom can hunt for her blessings on seeing her. And understanding about that circle of life is what triggered the man to go look for her. Not that she is too much of a woman or lady or something, when it comes to distinction with man by beauty. Of course, she could be a hot cake, which must be hunted for no doubt.

The Pretence of Love

The truth simply remains the same; successfully tricking her involves pretending to be in love with her (so that she gets carried away) and the bad guys are equal to the task. Until the container is empty—if care is not taken—no one leaves her. *"If a rat knew that danger encroached at its door, it would deny playing with the cat for a friendly relationship or even a wrestling contest."*

Some of the purposes might be that on different conditions she is beautiful or that she is financially buoyant. Another adage says, *"You use what you have to get what you want."* Sometimes you see or hear someone asking your woman if he can shop for her or even buy her a gift. Worst of all is when he asks her out for a food date.

Bewitched

The problem is that she's interested and glad enough to follow this guy without knowing the implications nor even bothering to seek your concept before exiting from the house. Besides, she also underrated you and such disregard is uncalled for and this kind of offence can change your mind-set into thinking that you are not man enough for her; that you are not in her priority and that she can won't respect you, even if you marry her in the nearest future.

The associated problem against such a lady is more or less spiritual. Powers can so round-core a lady, to the extent that she no longer has a say for herself. She just can't decide for herself and stand on it; never. May God deliver her.

In fact such a lady can become like a child who doesn't understand the implications of many things. For example, accepting food from somebody who seems ordinary, only to discover she's become bewitched and enslaved as his subject without options.

Evil offerings can purchase your rights (both spiritually and physically). Plus offerings that are wrongly accepted, can take you to where you never wanted to go and rob you of your blessings, if care is not taken. Also evil offerings can remote-control you so that you are caged in that battle of limitations, which may be the order of your days, if God does not intervene.

Only a Discussion was Offered to Eve

Evil offerings can also put on sparkling radiance, like the early morning sun, or like that of a golden object, just to induce you with certain attentions and stimulate your interest; inwardly it is dangerous to any mankind when taken or accepted. It could even be an evil satellite to watch your home and everything about you.

Someone could offer you anything just to be able to monitor your movement. Certain offers are projected to work to reduce your memory. All those offers are just to entice her in order to be able to change her programs and mentality to suiting their direction. When she is seen this time around her focus is lost, the real weapon is released now; then she can completely miss her target. Only a discussion was offered to Eve, she yielded in and also went in for it (Gen. 3:1-9). She completely lost her perfection and her entire generation's continuity in the same suffering.

This is the most inexplicable mistake, of the highest order, which brought Jehovah Himself to die for mankind. Can you imagine? Some races who know close to this fact hardly accept offerings, when they aren't too cleared with it. No matter their conditions, regarding what they know (and are culturally imparted and inclined), that some offers are dangerous; they can never accept what is questionable to them, as far as offerings are concerned.

Why was the evil fellow looking for her? Perhaps he was told about the history of her family background; how grounded it is with some notable recognition. And it also has financial reputation.

Everybody wants to identify with the famous. Who on earth doesn't want to identify with a reputable figure or family? So, as you can see such is a surety, which induces action for those desperately interested in a relationship with her, even though it is a total fake. In modern eras some evil guys who are fond of using ladies for fake businesses, will do anything to have the lady of their target, regardless of what it may cost them.

Ladies be Wise

They know that regardless of the final cost, they must gain. Due to much caring, the lady could get carried away; thinking that the guy is a true love. Ladies are so flexible in that they can easily fall victim if care is not taken. The way the world system is going, no one can really tell what is in the mind of evil people before that actually wreak their havoc on their targeted victims. Little did she know that what she called love is nothing but a dangerous business that could land her in disaster. Ladies be wise otherwise your supposed business with these fake personalities (to whom you are rather ignorant) will be a total flop.

Fake or mistaken love can be a vehicle that suspends the rider on the highway—a journey—to their destination. Bear that in mind. Fake love is a dilemma. Many have been used to promote evil or naughty business in the name of love. Your favourite lies in with certain danger if you aren't careful. Allurement is there. Ensnarement is also embedded. May God forbid it on your part in Jesus' name.

Overcoming the Evil Weapon of Pretension

"Look before you leap," is not fake advice. Many thought that those who were victimised must not have been sharp

enough. But take notice of those that take you out for flexing, pleasure and aggrandizement, for some are not genuine. Don't you rather think even when the ladies are wronged, they are still the ones begging, instead of a correction of error to be made. With that, the lady will get carried away into thinking that she is the *alpha* and *omega* not knowing that she is losing, and that problems encroach at her door. *"I am his pet can't you see!"* She says. But may you never be pet to untimely death, in Jesus' name.

Alternatively, a lady is not aware that she is about to lose certain virtues in her life, even her head. Before she knows of it, she will find herself where she didn't deserve. What a world! Pretension is one of the most dangerous weapons of the evil ones. Be alight in order to overcome their trickery.

C H A P T E R 6

Love of Husband

Married Life is Good

Matrimonial love is quite good. Primarily, even if it is the act of running helter-skelter in search for one or two minutes of love, it will save you of something. No hunter would like going to the bush every now and then if he can always find meat in his plate of soup and be left with enough to sell and to realise the sum. Similarly, as a single, let's for instance you used to watch ladies hot-jobs but behold, it is now even available at your disposal even natural, would you go search for one anymore? To me, no; not at all.

You can't tell me it has not saved such a one from the disgrace and embarrassment it causes, when after watching to get himself aroused and erect, (with no single one by his side), he burns with passion till dawn.

Advantages v Disadvantages

Married life is good. It saves many issues. But to every advantage there is equal and opposite disadvantage. If not the grace of God, on hearing the stories of those that are married, you will be afraid to even settle down. Those that are into it would be looking for somewhere to hide their heads, due to a lot of involvements. Talk of the responsibilities, which are another scary issue altogether. Kudos to every sincere married man and married woman, which are still in the marriage to date. God blesses you for real. May the grace of our Lord never leave you nor forsake you, in Jesus' name.

I tell you, to some extent love is a drama, look at what is going to happen here. The husband is the pride of a woman. We know that. Informally correct but in theory. Even he is a golden gown on her. He is her clothes and dignity. Very many to this end love to settle down for real. The respect it will yield her being in the midst of two consecutive families that already exist and have now come together as in-laws, is a big deal. Respect of a sister in-law, benefits and all that is like heaven right here on earth. On seeing the advantage of a matrimony the yearning interest is aroused in her.

Some women have over loved their husbands to the extent that they have gone the extra-mile to prove it to them by giving them girlfriends, even a second each. Some that are possessed with demonic power will bring their friends, even married, by luring their husbands to sleep with them, with the pretence of being unaware of what's going on. For example, if it is even worth doing at all, examining the intention of your lady or woman friend before you act.

Whosoever Spoils a Matrimony will be Spoiled Too

Don't be a spoiler to two in one. Some single ladies are looking forward to settling down and raising their families, while the bad ones who are already settled, are wasting their opportunities.

The good ones like to have families they can boldly call their own. The rational ones could reason that at a certain time in the future, somebody must take care of them when they are old (the children). It is high time they searched for their bus stop. Two good heads are better than one. And so, it is necessary to have a permanent caring personality around her she says. They can at least have a shift of responsibility. They want to have someone they can share ideas and plans with. The ultimate respect to any responsible woman is a real husband man.

Besides the normal thoughts as mentioned above, which sound so reasonable, there are some riff-raff ladies who will also prefer a married man. A sugar daddy for money and fun has consequences at the end for your information. These sets would allow the devil to use them in order to scatter marriages (Matt. 19:6). Why?

You can imagine such an important figure with dignity; what his wife can't tell him at home, a small girl (whom he's old enough to father), can say it to him and even have her way with it. What a demonic golden privilege!

The most surprising thing is that the chief will still be the first to call her and start begging with money and promises of one thing or the other. They are so demonic, even privileged that they could conk the men which any of them can't have his wife tried that to him at home, else, that is the day the woman gets to her father's compound.

Not all Monkeys that eat Banana make a Noise

Let us talk about some of the reasons why so many single ladies prefer married men as friends for sexual relationships. They do it because they feel that they got the experience in bed and so they could also take care of them with maturity and care for them for real, with financial support and others ways, but in a silent tone. It is true that not all monkeys that eat banana make noise.

No lady wants what she does in secrete to be aired in public. Likewise the man would not want his wife to know of it, plus the lady wouldn't want anybody knowing that she's dating a married man. 1. Her life is in danger with the wife of whom she is dating, 2. Her reputation is finished publicly if it escalates. The disadvantage also is that, they wouldn't have as much time to spend together like in the case of a single guy. Yet she goes for a married man because of both his physical and spiritual money.

CHAPTER 7

Love of Wife

Marriage to the Proper Rib is Complete

Historically, it was foretold that something left the side of a man; to date he is still looking for what left him and which rendered him incomplete as a single person, until after marriage to the proper rib. You see, a man today is not a complete man, when he is not married. God proved it first. Where He saw that Adam needed a *"help meet"* and that living alone was not ideal for him. He made Eve to support him if not for any other thing; at least to share ideas and plans together. Adam really cherished her when she was actually presented to him (Gen. 2:18, 23-25).

So, today a man likes a woman whenever he sets his eyes on her because she is a wooer and a *"help meet"* for good.

But what matters most is the right rib. So, it's neither a knew thing nor a crime, to start searching for the right woman (when the right time comes for it). But it is a pity that bad people in our society today, mostly step into a relationship with a focus on married women. One may begin to wander, *"Why married women when single ladies and girls are wondering aimlessly and excessively all over the globe?"* This is a demonic ministry assigned to them; in order to turn the already married women — settled in their matrimonial homes — into spare tyres to some one else's vehicle. I would advise that it is actually a syndrome in our society with all it's imperfections.

Ingredients

Any lady who wants to live a decent matrimonial life with her husband (without any error), must settle anything necessary in her life before settling down with her life partner. Remember this is the reason why we have what is called ingredients. I believe somebody can get me cleared of what I am trying to marshal out here. Avoid that beast and powers and come to Jesus, He will settle you for good.

The fact that human life is two or even more, does not mean we should be crazy. They forgot one thing that the bible says, *"Thou shall not put asunder whatsoever God has joined together"* (Matt. 19:6). It is alarming lately the rate at which couples are broken up in their matrimonies. It was supposed to sacred, something to honour and respect for real, to God's glory. Culturally, it is also recognized as a precept ordained as a pattern by Him.

Avoid Laying your Eggs in Many Baskets

God is very much interested in matrimony. It interests Him to see men fulfilling His ordination with a command, which has all kinds of blessings attached to it (Gen. 1:28). 1. A man is looking for his side rib. 2. He wants to fulfil his complete manhood. As stated in (Gen. 1:28) which is a must to every mankind dwelling under the sun. But don't go about multiplying into different homes and think that you are doing it correctly. Please, avoid laying your eggs in many baskets, on the basis of matrimony. God did not approve that to any woman or man.

An excellent wife is also a sparkling jewel on the crown of the man. She is worthy and reliable. Her husband is a man of confidence. They both can defeat any trouble or battle that confronts them or come their way. She is cherished and acceptable by the husband (Gen. 2:23).

Despite the dignity attached to a married woman, some unfaithful ones, with irresponsible character, still accept some crossover, (like some single ladies without control), based on what they belonged to before their matrimonies. Those things which they could not settle before marriage and as a result continue keeping extra-marital affairs with men as attachments to their husbands.

Moreover, when they also want to lay foundations for their children, in the second part of human life, they can also engage. This is actually the moment you begin to see a housewife getting attracted to single bad guys and some foolish men who have allowed powers to soiled their minds into hunting for women in their matrimonial homes. The truth of the matter is that both sides know what they are doing and searching for.

For example, a man going through this, in his matrimony with his partner, does not even need external bodies to help him monitor his wife; without even the help from a prophet he can easily notify it from her movement, talk and conversation. No matter how she may try to conceal her secrecy in the act of cheating, she must be notified.

Her Retaliation

"No person can put two palm-fruits in his or her mouth rolling to and fro and yet having a clear voice in his or her conversation." Check her make-up, if you are disciplined and rational, you see questionability written. Sometimes, if they are given money for shopping, they halve it and save part of it, in order to take care of their boyfriends; that is if they don't work. Similarly, they can as well tax their husbands for money and when denied they starve their husbands in bed, as punishment or retaliation.

They can condition them and even pressurise them with excuses to want to buy this and that; meanwhile they have already targeted who is going to benefit from the money at last, which is known by them. The same thief who sees and benefits the intestine of the whole thing will still get paid at the end of the day. Pets she just can't give her husband, she will fully give to a thief. What a life!

Marriage is a complete mistake and a complete fake, by laying a total claim of property, which does not belong only to you. The human question is why marriage? Is it culturally an obligation to fulfil or what? The fact is that, in human view of the practical effect on both sides, there is no 100% positive reflection of what it is expected. Imagine something a husband has paid for, even before the parents and family people of the bride—also in the eyes of the entire world—is now being denied of him.

Without Rocking the Boat of Another

When the man is late, you see her using it to beg for men out there, even some young bad guys that are not worth the standard of her own late husband, and she is even old enough to birth their age mate. May the good God help us in Jesus' name. Why? Life is a perversion in the hand of mankind, under demonic influence.

Secrete intelligent battles are fighting men, unknown to the world. Modern or no modern era, God is seriously against any act of crossing for another, whereby you have your own and even when you don't yet have. He has even placed a choice down for any man who finds such being done to his boat, can decide whether to let go with forgiveness or file for a divorce (Matt. 5:32). No matter what is in her that you like, there are more than a million just like that in the world; you must find your own freed single without having to rock the boat of another.

CHAPTER 8

Love of Children

Reproduction

At a certain time and age in life, one will begin to desire children. It is naturally an obligation for one to reproduce, in order to fulfil the ordination of our Sovereign Lord. This is one of the reasons why you see some ladies sleep with dolls, when the right husband is yet to come in their lives; in their closets just to feel what looks like a baby to them, not merely guys or men.

They are naturally free gifts from God (Ps. 127:3). They are caring when they grow up. They even serve their parents freely from childhood to adult. Some parents just like to give birth to children because they want to multiply and also want to know what their replica will look like; that's all. They never thought of the care, which is important and involved in the whole matter.

Informed or Deformed?

That is why some children are wayward because they lacked informal education from their biological parents. *"When you are not informed you are deformed."* Imagine a fowl laying her eggs without incubating and hatching them, what would that look like? Do you still wait for me to tell you the origin of the nuisance in our society? Parents just want the continuation of the name of their lineage. That's all; any other thing doesn't concern them.

The fact that Jehovah God said in (Gen. 1:28) go into the world and multiply doesn't mean you should give birth to pose problems on the world or government. If you give birth without being catered for, it is a problem on the rest people of the entire world, due to the collective responsibility of human nature. Bad children are a complete problem to the nation of their origin; believe it or not. This is because, a child is a leader of tomorrow. Behold, children are a heritage from the Lord and the fruit of the womb a reward (Ps. 127:3).

The womb of a woman can carry eminent personalities. You can begin by naming them as apostles, prophets, evangelists, pastors and teachers in God's vineyard; doctors, judges, professors, inventors, sailors, pilots, drivers, engineers, lecturers, pop-stars, supper-stars, actors, authors, presidents, governors, kings and queens, prominent business personalities just to mention a few.

Her Womb is the Target

You can see that the womb of a woman is blessed. There is no doubt why the devil attacks her so much; so that she doesn't fulfil her ministry.

On the contrary, some people do not like to have children even when they are married. They believe that children are a disturbance. Some are even afraid to go into it because they are confused and just don't know what to do. Don't be afraid because, *"If the boldness to face danger were determined by size, a mosquito couldn't be reckoned with!"* Have a positive mind-set and go into it; success is your portion in Jesus' name.

Then there are those who believe in the notion that having children can pose stress, such that they can hardly have time for themselves. It is indeed a task, which does not deserve human reward nor does it earn you with any payment or income. For that reason, the interest is not humanly available, but you can imagine them selling the above in the spiritual realm. What a world!

Yet these people fail to realize that having children is the very first ministry of mankind—since Genesis—from God. And if you do it well and the glory goes to God, He will never fail to rain down blessings on you—as far as His assignment to man is concerned.

If therefore you ask, *"How is the ministry?"* You may be thinking that it only has to do with ministering in the pulpit on the podium. Or better still, preaching as a shepherd to the fold of God, for the welfare of His flock. Capitally no.

Awake! Awake! All is well when you Involve God

Anything you do is your ministry. It is a part of what you will account for on the day of reckoning. So I dare someone to awake in his or her mind and do the correct thing. Awake! Awake! Awake from slumber somebody. God is your strength. It may not be humanly possible by you, but with God all things are possible. Although, there could be challenges along the way (based on the responsibilities involved in matrimony), never mind, it is well when you involve God.

This issue is on a voluntary basis, as we've discussed, so far in the above subject. But we also have what is called involuntary birth. This refers to those who desire to have children but are denied. There are many reasons behind this fact. There can be forces at work over them, in order not to have children. If that be the case, somebody suffering from this problem needs deliverance. If they are not set free they can't fulfil this ministry. It could be inherited or a foundational problem but it doesn't matter which, the most important thing it that it's gotten rid of by the help of God.

God Introduced Himself at the Level of His Capacity

To this end, God has introduced Himself at the level of His capacity to resolve the problems of mankind, which was are humanly impossible or incurable (Jer. 32:27). This is not just a mere spoken word, rather a word that carries power from the very mouth of His Divinity, to effect positive results in the lives of those concerned. We have seen the cases of Sarah and Hannah in the bible, where God intervened in their situations of barrenness and fake names.

Remember, Hannah called the God of solutions into her situation. What about you? Do you think it is impossible with God? Don't think like that. The fact that God has not granted favour to your positive requests doesn't mean He hasn't heard you. He is carefully working on your case systematically—in accordance with His timetable. You will smile in some days. You will take and proclaim that day to be the *best ever,* because of the answer to your prayers. He is a miracle worker. A prayer answering God. Unchangeable changer and unmovable mover. That God is still very much alive. He still can do it for you (what can be both seen and felt) and you will testify to His glory. Hallelujah!

Embrace the Chief of Solutions to become Immune

Another problem, which can make some people to suffer barrenness, is too much abortion. Ambitions have made many single ladies who fornicate around to abort babies too much that, on arrival they can no longer have any; their womb is already damaged. If you are such a fellow, all hope is not lost. I dare you to summon up courage by faith and tap from God, through Jesus the Author and finisher of our faith.

Ask for God's mercy. Come to Jesus Who can give a womb to those that have lost theirs to abortion and terrible diseases and afflictions. Quack doctors have caused a lot of damage to the wombs of their victims. In summary, whether you caused your own problems or someone else did, Christ the Chief of solutions is available and at your disposal. Embrace Him and get immune; God blesses you.

CHAPTER 9

Love of Education & Student

The Key to Success

Basically, there is informal education whereby parents teach and impart into their children; the ways of life based on societal conformity. On this foundation, parents fully rest their confidence that their children can never yield any reproach. And any parent who neglects this responsibility (especially at the earlier stages), can never have rest of mind. Rather they are expecting one bad news after another, due to lack of confidence on their children.

Besides informal education, the next thing that responsible parents can give to their children is formal education. Not just education but quality education with ideal knowledge, which can never be taken from them, but help them to be somewhere in the prospect.

Knowledge & Quality Education is Power

Education is the key to success. They say knowledge is power, it is indeed a true saying. The best that rational parents can give to their children, is nothing but a quality education. Almost everybody likes it and it's worth delighting in because it makes them to be part of the productive people of the world. Without doubt, if you are a well educated person, you are already economically productive in your own right. It brings idea for one to operate with. And at the long run, it is a pleasure, which can make one catch fun.

Today, technology is number one in the world, apart from nature. It brings development. And education can make you travel around the world to interact with people of different races, with good expressions and shared experiences.

Education has brought many advancements in the world, day in and day out. Due to this fact, universities are producing technical know-how, with great ideas that have the potential to change this world for the better. Education is good, yet good manners shouldn't ever be neglected. They are both interwoven. And when the two are completed, the education system is balanced in the life of individual. And that makes him or her a learned or renowned person. If peradventure one is lagging, then it's usually proven by one's rudeness.

Illiteracy is the brother of arrogance and lawlessness and they both come as a result of the lack of education. The simple fact is that uneducated fellows can never listen to advice or suggestions — the way that they ought to — because they've never been so inclined (to sit in the four corners of a classroom and be teachable).

Love of Student

A student is anybody who is ready and willing to learn, whether in a classroom setting or open air, in order to listen and receive a lesson from a tutor or teacher. Those who are teachable desire to learn (whether formally or informally), provided there's knowledge and skills to be acquired. But it is a pity that those who are ready, don't always have link, while those lackadaisical fellows are into opportunities they can never appreciate.

Some people want to learn in order to become somebody but lack someone who will train or teach them with what they need to know. What a life! Orphans are more or less an example of this. While many children with lively parents, will deliberately refuse to go to school nor want to listen to any parental advice; whereas orphans are willing—at any length—but lack the teachers necessary.

The responsible ones will say, *"If I can learn to become somebody, I shall be very much okay."* Some will be very serious with their lives and education, yet have no sponsor. Even if they're very intelligent, there's still no help coming from anywhere. The children of the simple, know that if you are knowledgeable, you can easily find a better job and earn good money. Better still, you can even be self-employed. It's known around the world, that people are proud (with good or bad pride), only once they've acquire education.

We observed technically, that many students are very rich when they are still schooling. The secrete behind this fact is that they used the medium of student-hood to extort money from their parents, even when they are not asked to pay for anything in the schools. As far as the parents may not have access nor even taken time to ask, they succeed and go away with it.

Opportunity, Responsibility & Leadership

Many ignorant parents are living deaths due to this fact because, their children have stripped them financially. Some are even living on debt. May the good God help us in Jesus' name. Since they are not the one responsible for their schooling, they don't usually feel the pain, as far as they are not the direct persons making the money with which they go to school.

Some are very lucky with good relatives who show good interest concerning their academic pursuits. Students have access to so many people, from all walks of life and as a result, they are bound to have as many friends as possible. That of course can easily give birth to popularity. With knowledge of education, you can handle responsibilities and even take up any leadership position.

A graduate of political science can decide to register a political party, in order to be voted for. And if it happens that he or she wins, he can automatically become a leader. So, priority of leadership can even make people like education.

As a student, you have a certain authority vested in you by the federal government, which covers you in case of any violations of law and order, so that you can be considered to some extent by the law.

Love to study good things and not evil, for education is good. That is why you hear a criminal student is considered with certain draconian measures against a crime. Do not abuse the privilege, else you go in for it.

Chapter 10

Love of Teacher

The Impartation of Knowledge is a Big Deal

A student can never be a student without a teacher and a teacher can never be a teacher without a student, to demonstrate his or her profession. Imparting knowledge into others is a big deal. Teaching as a profession is also a ministry.

A teacher is a father or a mother of technology; who teaches in order to raise up students with both technical know-how and great potential; with ideas to change the world for a better position. A teacher simply teaches what he or she knows, in order to impart the concerned with the appropriate knowledge. It is either natural, artificial or by training.

Some teachers love teaching for different reasons. For example before one chooses a career, one must already have gotten some knowledge of it, in order to see whether or not it's full of advantage or disadvantage and whether it's worth going for or not. A student knows that with advantages it is positive, therefore can go for it as a teacher. And so, a teacher is a personality who is exposed to many people of different races, societal-classes, levels, backgrounds, education (informal/formal), beauty, ideas, focus, and so forth.

The Temptations of a Teacher

In human society, we all know that there are temptations. But it is not very good to spoil your seed or building. How can you be teaching students and at the same time be befriending them for sex? Even if it is good to have an affair, outside your profession or ministry is better. Which saves or secures your name. Secondly, you can also protect your seed in the students by not having anything to do with them on the basis of affair.

Take for instance, you end up impregnating the only daughter to her parents in secondary school and whereby the parents are already aged; worse of all, you have not the intention to marrying her, I therefore leave you to judge yourself. And her parents may even hope on her to be their bread winner in the nearest future. Oh, what a deep blow you have caused that family? It is bad agriculture to plant seeds, which you later intend to spray with chemicals in order to kill the crop. I don't think you are one of them. Are you? You have not only succeeded in ruining a generation but naturally you have changed the first target and purpose, by so doing in her.

The fact that you have the opportunity to access so many beautiful girls doesn't mean you are entitled to sleep with them all. Remember you are going to account for it man. Are you so legalised? You aren't. They were brought to you so that you could teach them; so teach them, for they already belong to others.

How do you enjoy sexual actions, carried out on a table in the office during school hours? If not for a demonic assignment, would it be interesting and partially enjoyable to you, based on what you are enticed?

Exonerated from his Constant Bullying

From one profession, you now find yourself doing two, which you made out of demonic choices. The aftermath and reward, is it good or bad? Who knows whether or not that particular girl (whose vehicle of academic pursuit you attacked with sex), would be a minister that the nation would need, as a saviour for moving forward in the prospect.

Many girls fall into fake relationships with male teachers, mostly because he is jovial, handsome, intelligent, influential and popular. Out of much bullying and prejudice, a single girl in school could be forced into a relationship with a male teacher. She yields, only to save herself or be exonerated from his constant bullying.

It can also happen whereby the girl is not that intelligent but would want to pass his paper in order to cure her shame before her parents who suppose that she's not that serious about school. Every dull student wants to impress their people, even if means faking exam results, he or she is ready to do it.

We all know that some parents are very particular about how much their children are grounded in the acquisition of knowledge. In fact, how serious the children are taking their studies, is often their greatest concern. And if their grades are not up to scratch, or at a satisfactory level, such parents can easily stop them from schooling.

Alternatively, they might be asked to do learning work, which they may never like. They wouldn't want to miss their friends. Dropping out of school half way can mean also a withdrawal from many opportunities. And so, to avoid facing such humiliation, (compounded with multiple peer pressures), they must do anything possible to position themselves before it's too late.

May God Pardon your Crimes against their Destinies

When a male teacher wants to gain ground in a strange community (of his newly posted place), he can decide to befriend any indigent as a student in his class. However, to interact in a culture with people of a new place (as a teacher), does not necessitate you befriending their daughter in your teaching class, whereby you know that you can never marry her tomorrow. Look, it is a total pretension of you and only you know of this.

Some highly demonically inclined female teachers seduce some young boys in schools and thereby ruin their careers. What a shame! May God pardon your crimes against their destinies. If that was how you were attacked, you wouldn't attain your giant or stage. Many guys who were actually boasting about their ambition ended up becoming totally nothing as a result of this. *"Shoes,"* they say, *"have sizes."* Please, go for your class and leave people's children alone.

Every element you can see with breath has a responsibility. I understand, that some guys are really attractive and handsome to the core. But that does not mean you should lust to the extent you can't control yourself anymore.

Fear God & don't do Such a Thing

Condescending to befriending a student boy in your class is a complete corruption. Check it out yourself. Consider the gap between the both of you. Primarily, you have gone so very far, while he is just a beginner, who doesn't know anything pertaining to life. I do believe if you are rational, you can tell how many rivers he still has to cross. Do you know that if a lie becomes a reality, a liar cannot identify because of shame?

That is exactly what I am trying to say. A situation whereby you are to really introduced to each other for a marriage, you just can't. You find out that you will be ashamed (or not even willing) because you are too old for him. If love is sweet, all through I would say it is a done issue. If having an affair is good; please not with your student.

Okay, why didn't you befriend one of your co-teachers? At least, that should be fairly good to the sight, but not your student whose future is just like an egg (as far as school or career is concerned) under your responsibility over him. If you had the fear of God, you wouldn't have done such a thing.

C H A P T E R 11

Intellectual Love

Lasting Legacy

Intellectual ability is worth delighting over. When you have it, you have gotten one of life's major solutions. Including a key to the door of opportunity; those of which you never imagined possible.

Education induces discovery of invention, which helps to change the world for a better position. It attracts respect to intellects by those who know the value. And these sets of people are also regarded as public figures and are well recognised in society.

Their case is indelible in the memory of mankind. They are easily remembered with the legacy they leave with men when they are gone and that makes their spirits continue to live among men. As they have made impart in the lives of people. You just can't beat them in their field and if care is not taken, they are even consultants in the circle. The bible says, "God is the giver of knowledge of craft-man-ship" (Ex. 31:3).

Love of Illiteracy

This is the inability to read and write. Can you imagine, while many are striving to acquire knowledge and skills to be useful, there's others who prefer to remain illiterate, due to some reasons you'll never know, except they be unveiled to you. Knowledge they say is power. It is indeed. But we cannot really tell why someone would leave it and choose to remain illiterate for the rest of their lives.

For example, when one's helper dies and there's no longer any provision or means to provide for oneself; then it can happen. Or when parents are too poor and no one to help, it can also happen. When there is a spiritual threat against one about it, it can happen most especially when one has no means to battle in order to avert it, it can happen. And when one doesn't know Jesus, whereby the enemy can mesmerise one, it can also happen. May God help us.

When one is not meeting up with one's academic standard, one can willingly stop or be stopped by one's parents instead of pretending to have one's parents to continue to waste their money for nothing. If you are the fashionable type, it can also happen. You see your mates wearing the best clothes and caching fun without taking time to find out how; you give up your education and jump along with them; you have chosen to be a complete and future illiterate in the prospect.

The Mother of Illiteracy

Laziness or reluctance towards facing challenges (or studying thoroughly in order to acquire the best of knowledge), is the mother of illiteracy. They just can't make do with their brain along with their mates. A man sometimes could be whatever he chooses to be (Prov. 23:7). As the saying goes, *"What we cannot avoid, at least we have to endure it."* Hence he or she has no choice, due to poverty, except perhaps stealing or engaging in bad business, for survival.

Whether or not school is declared free by the federal government, you still must buy school materials, uniforms, and sandals, and finally take on the consideration of mobility, to reach there at the allotted times. And so, all these involve cash, which when not available can make you reconsider your plans as beating the air, as far as education is concerned.

There are certain cultures and traditions on royal titles, which may not permit an exit from the kingdom for the sake of education. Therefore, anybody in this situation has relatively no permission to go to school, other than to adjust to the system practiced by their forefathers and when violated this results in instantaneous death without mercy. Ancient traditional practices have certain calamities attached to them, in the case of any violations, such that can easily call the people to order (for a correction against a disaster).

Similarly, if the community that one hails from has a very powerful juju that the people serve as their religion and which is strongly believed in by the people. For example, taking care of it is seen as a great obligation that cannot be shifted to another person, lest one might be restricted and not be allowed to go to school at all.

In fact if there is a denied responsibility by the next of kin, the entire family must perish from the community at large (both home and abroad) including the person in question. Therefore no one is implored by anybody to be the successor as priest (taking up his duty) as they can't do anything to avert it. Especially if there's no alternate sacrifice to appease to the gods, for a solution.

The Consequences of COVID-19 on Education

When a family or an individual is cursed against education they can also hate going to school. COVID-19 has discouraged so many of the younger generations from going to school. The year 2020 is a dramatic history in the life of the entire human race, we all will never forget. That is simply because the interest has long been killed by powers. Except God intervenes there's no remedy. If he or she does not know God through genuine repentance and confessed on Jesus Christ, he is bound to remain illiterate forever without knowing his left from his right.

When he or she can't break free, they begin to like it by force. When one is spiritually dull, one finds it so very difficult to know the truth from error; because one's understanding is being blocked or blindfolded by the enemy. In (Matt. 6:33) the bible says, *"Seek first the kingdom of God and His righteousness and every other things shall be added unto you."* It is indirectly telling you to have God or Jesus in your life, then God will make you have and enjoy everything that He carried within

Himself and along with Himself into your life. *"It is well with me,"* somebody says. Amen.

CHAPTER 12

Love for God

Wholeheartedness

If you hate air for example, you will die. But I thank God for He is much more than that. He created even the air and gave us freely to consume without any demand of payment. If air were to be a prepaid-card and you failed to recharge it, you can imagine what would happen to you. You would immediately suffocate.

"Love the Lord your God with all your heart, with all your soul and with all your mind" (Matt. 22:37).

A round of applause to God who did not see this to be His source of income to enrich Himself. So, you can't just evade your Creator overnight. He is so indispensable in everything. You can see, it is too late now to quit just like that. As you need Him, you need to also love Him, it is what you love that yields you with a positive result. Consider the hatred you have for death, does it really yield to you with any positive result? Of course not.

Take for instance if oxygen where to be paid for, how would it be with mankind? If the locomotive ability we are naturally endowed with, were to be paid for, you couldn't move unless you could afford the payment. What about the power of service, I mean the energy with which all of us utilise to embark on our day today activities of life in search for bread? Then you cannot venture into any form of endeavour, which yields income as your means of surviving lively-hood.

Praise His Great Kindness

Can you pay for human telephones and then think of the natural means of communication; the mouth and the sound it produces. You can converse or discuss now till tomorrow and no one bills you. My friend, is it worthy to give the Lord God a praise? Yes it is. And I at this juncture can help you out with a praise to the Lord that cares in Jesus' name. Please, appreciate God for His kind gesture towards mankind.

Can you see the rate at which children are being aborted? What about you? You could have been aborted the same way but nay, God protected you till you were delivered with safety. God blesses you. What of your wisdom and knowledge with senses of humour that the Lord God allowed you to consume freely without any form of payment? Oh, the Lord is actually good for His mercy endures forever.

Praise His Infinite Mercy

Can you see, feel and even experience God in His infinite mercy, which endures forever? Please, I dare you to give God a holy praise and worship. This is very much necessary as an appreciation to Him. In recognition of His work and miracles that money cannot buy; give Him endless praise and worship, they are His only food. Well done Jehovah.

Think of other examples or behold every natural endowment that the Lord God has given us to enjoy the world; before it is due for us to return to Him. His continual caring for us is worth millions more than the care of humans and even parents. As our divine landlord and the author and finisher of our faith, He is actually doing His marvellous work over us. May His name be praised.

Beloved, won't you rather think that this God is worthy to be praised and respected to the core? And so, for you to respect God, you need nothing other than to love Him and keep His commandments and treat others right with the genuine love of Christ. He does not even need your money. But don't deny Him off His praises and worship. I mean, holy praise and worship with every capacity to fulfilling the destiny of mankind to the glory of God (Ps. 150).

Let your careers, your duties, your position, your job, your businesses, your marriages, your productiveness, your travelling, your homes and properties, your beauty, your colours, your clothing, your manners, your approaches, your benevolence, your laughter, your smiles and your discussions; your leadership, your laws, your advice, your teachings and preaching, your unions etc., give God a complete praise to His holy name in Jesus' name.

With Holy Passion

You could be good, yet the bible says we should never forsake the assembly of the righteous (Heb. 10:25). Endeavour to go to church always, in order to be able to identify and maintain your salvation by retaining your integrity and ground in Him. Beloved, in a nutshell, I shall be glad to see you embraced by Christ as a heavenly candidate.

Do not be a merely bible scripted person, rather practice everything it entails to be a good Christian to the end. As a heavenly ambassador, remember we all as believers have a home that the hand of man did not build; so, work towards it with a holy passion. God blesses you. See you there. On a human level, we all know that it is completely impossible but with God it is quite possible in Jesus' name.

CHAPTER 13

Love of Holiness & Prayers

Love of Holiness

To be reckoned with by God is a great pleasure. Job was reckoned with by God. This is an act of the practising saint to the glorification of God. To everything that a man does, there is a reason. Holy love is possible when one is heavenly conscious and also inclined with it. And this is one of the qualities God requires of those who serve Him.

He said, I am Holy; therefore, those that worship me must do that in spirit and in truth (John 4:23-24). Secondly, God has said that our body is the temple of the indwelling Holy Spirit (1 Cor. 6:19). And where there is the Holy Spirit, God dwells in there. You are freed from troubles, because of the freedom which God's presence grants.

Holiness Attracts God

Our iniquity induces a shortness of blessings from God. Due to this fact, people decide to practice holiness in order to stimulate or attract the attention of God and be blessed by Him. If you hide transgressions, the Lord God will never hear you. But thanks be to God for the way out that He provided, as a solution. The fervent prayers of a righteous man avail much in the sight of God.

As sin brings hindrance to our prayers, they should also disgust us — as they disgust God — if we don't want any delays on our blessings. In everything we do, there should be an atom of holiness and a genuine cordial relationship with God.

A carnal man can never understand the things of the Spirit. If you are therefore holy, God can always reveal things to you and you will see things clearly. Sin can blind you spiritually, even when your enemy is operating you can never know. Sin can make you so very confused, such that you can hardly distinguish dreams. It takes light to illuminate darkness for visibility to clearance. The purpose for which the Word of God (Jesus who is also the light) came was for our enlightenment. Jesus brought a holy civilization to us. Therefore, the door of salvation is opened to many.

The question is who has this holy love to express towards his or her neighbour? Not on this planet can anyone be found with this heart of gold or of God. The simple fact is that human beings have long fallen, many years ago, before the era of Jesus (B.C.) let alone this dispensation of the Holy

Spirit (A.D.). Move very close to any fellow — a believer that speaks with other tongues — and you will discover that they have notable weak-points in some issues. To the point that you can't come any closer due to how much you are disgusted by such a character.

God can't Hear the Political Ritualist

Human beings are fighting battles right from when imperfection incarnated. There is nothing that will make flies caste a vote for a healthy person, not even without sores. Food we all know preserves life for real. There's no single living creature that is not aware of this fact. And so, be informed, that hunger is worse than an epidemic. There's no government, of any nation, that doesn't budget and make allocation to fight hunger. If you can fight hunger, you have succeeded in fighting half of your problems. As it is with the individual, so it is with the government, trust me.

Your mind as a civilian thinks that governments do not pray. Be it believing or unbelieving governments, they all do pray, in order to avert one problem or another. Only the Lord God can tell the kind of prayers they pray at every point in time.

Remember, it is written that the prayer of a sinner is an abomination to God (Prov. 28:9). Therefore, if anybody is a political ritualist, God can't hear them. Their prayers are in vain and the situation cannot change throughout their regime. This is one of the reasons that governments battle with too many problems. Because if you are not good, you can never get any goodness. It takes good things, to get good things.

Love of Prayers

Prayer is a communication or an expression of one's feelings or demands over one or two things. As far as our Master is concerned, our Lord Jesus Christ has defined and demonstrated to us what prayer is all about and how to pray. He has demonstrated to us, the holy foundation of prayers that we all must pray for these end times.

We noticed that before He requested anything from God for us, He first thanked God (Luke 9:16). For our prayers to be answered, we were also told by Jesus to forgive one another by simply praying our Lord's prayer:

"Our Father, which art in heaven, hallowed be thy name. Thy kingdom come. Thy will be done in earth, as it is in heaven. Give us this day our daily bread. And forgive us our debts, as we forgive our debtors. And lead us not into temptation, but deliver us from evil: for thine is the kingdom, and the power and the glory, forever. Amen" (Matt. 6:9-13).

That was the foundational requirement of prayer to God. Right now in heaven, Jesus is still interceding in order for us to make eternity, which He worked for us with His precious blood on the cross of cavalry. Who knew no sin and took upon Himself the iniquity of the entire world and nailed it to the cross. Where He actually declared it was finished and that whosoever believes, salvation belongs to them. Hallelujah.

There were so many characters in the bible who prayed and the Lord God answered. Abraham prayed for Abimelech;

the affliction that was a warning to him and the members of his household — for keeping Sarah in his custody — was averted. He also prayed on behalf of his nephew Lot and the Lord God answered him and granted favour on his requests. Plus, Moses prayed on several occasions, where the power of God demonstrated in answer to the demands of His people, the Israelites.

Baptised through the Waters of the Red Sea

Jehovah never really failed His part to take good care of Israel, with full answers that showed His concern for their situations. We saw it at the Red Sea; where the waters was divided for the people of God to pass through to dry land. Take this as a lesson to benefit you; your enemies can't swim and that's why the Lord God made you pass through your own Red Sea situation. They can't taste your kind of experiences. They can't sit in your kind of class of destiny and take your lessons. They just can't receive the authenticity of your lessons. You are just too far from their standard.

We saw how the Lord God actually demonstrated His awesomeness and even baptised the Israelites, while taking them across the Red Sea. That's an area too mysterious for us without the help of a theologian or the Holy Spirit.

We also saw God answer through the water from the rock that satisfied the thirsting Israelites in the desert. Moses also pleaded with God for mercy on behalf of the Israelites that He intended to destroy because of their disobedience.

When the Israelites warred against their enemies under the leadership of Moses, God also answered Moses as he was praying with the elders of Israel, for victory over their enemies (Ex. 17:12). Finally the Lord God hearkened to Moses prayers for Joshua his successor.

Jephthah asked the Lord God to let the sun stand still until he defeated his enemies. God favoured him even though he vowed to burn as an offering the first thing that came out of his home (ironically his only daughter). Glory to God who equally gives and takes away; may His name be praised.

Bitter made Sweet through Answered Prayers

Esther fasted and prayed in order to meet the king on behalf of the Israelites and the supposed protocol of the king Ahasuerus was defied for her sake; then she found favour with the king (Est. 2:17). Daniel prayed and the mouths of the lions were stopped for his sake. Prophet Elijah prayed and there was no rain for three years, as he asked, the Lord God answered immediately by granting favour to his request.

Elisha prayed in Jericho that the waters would be purified. In addition Joshua, David, Amos, Ezekiel, Paul and Timothy, all prayed and the Lord God answered them. Prophet Samuel pleaded to God for king Saul and he was shown mercy.

The pioneers of Pentecostalism: the first apostles of Jesus, among whom was Peter, who prayed for a blind beggar at the beautiful gate, to regain his sight and to His glory God answered. Uncountable hosts of others prayed to God and God did not fail to answer them for His glory in Jesus' name.

Beloved, your prayer is not in vain; keep it up the Lord God will see you through. For you to be very sure, the Lord God has said that you should watch having prayed. The reason He has said you should watch is that the answers will definitely come. God blesses you.

CHAPTER 14

Love of Light

Evil Runs from the Light

Light is indeed worthy of delight. When God created the heavens and the earth, everywhere was empty yet full of darkness; until He invoked the light. That was why Jesus said, *"I am the light."* When light comes, darkness will disappear. It also symbolises truth, goodness, honesty, consideration and love for one another, which is actually done from the bottom of a holy heart of gold where the Lord God is involved.

He who loves light, loves God, for He is light. Light can give you a road to breakthrough. Evil runs from light. It reveals to you where there are loopholes in your life. It is also a symbol of righteousness. Light can correct errors and omissions. Wisdom — as a solution to a problem — can be considered light. Knowledge is also a light.

It may not merely be the physical light made by human hands or the natural light in the enclosure, rather your doings towards one another. Some people are just generous, benevolent and kind. Their common interest is to see that it is also well with others. They can never embark on silly things against their neighbours. They love to do good and make peace for the sake of God, for simplicity is their target and focus.

God Protects the Simple

If you want truth in anything and you go to them, they will tell you nothing but the simple truth straight away. They are ever ready to teach people what they know, even when it comes to copying their knowledge, they just don't mind teaching you. But don't abuse their kindness, else God will fight you, for God protects the simple (Ps. 116:6). Never abuse or embarrass a humble character that comes to you with a good motive. Many have mistakenly offended and driven away their angels.

Ask me who is going to defend them and help them in many ways? May such a mistake never be our lot or portion in Jesus' name.

We all know that everybody cannot be a messiah, it is not possible. To do good has to do with what is in your heart. I want to ask you a simple question, which could sound embarrassing to your hearing. It can tickle even the ear of a bad listener, who never expected such a dangerous question. To such, compliance to human conformity is not in him or her at all. There is no way negative can produce positive, never, it's not possible. You know it is unarguably that all of us reason differently and most of our reasons are full of doses. That's for the ordinary human imperfection.

However what if one is full of witchcraft and their demon is yet to be removed for example, *"Evil members in the body" (Matt. 10:36)?* If it were possible that each of us were to unveil their parcel in the mind, you just couldn't stand the missile of some of us. I tell you. The scientists are not fools. They experimented on human beings and came up with a name: *animals with complex brains, with the ability to reason and carry it out in action.*

Destruction Starts in the Mind

Therefore, a human cannot just do anything without reasoning, which means whatever a man does, it's a baby birthed from the mind.

If you must kill, if you must cheat, if you must deceive, if you must trick, if you must lure, if you must mislead, if you must misguide, if you must destroy, if you must kidnap, if you must fail, if you must disappoint, if you must disgrace, if you must humiliate, if you must reproach, if you must conspire, if you must castigate, if you must betray, if you must lie, if you must fornicate, if you must commit adultery, if you must rob, if you must create asunder between couples, if you must spoil a relationship, if you must bewitch anybody's child, if you must sleep with somebody's wife, if you must spoil, if you must build, and so on and so forth, you must first plan it from the mind.

So, be careful how you use your mind so that it does not lead you to destruction. The heart of man is a battle centre for Satan against the will of God for mankind. The purpose is to make man go against their will and purpose by God.

God has a pattern for man to live a better life. It was the devil who tricked man to make the wrong choice, which led them into problems. May God's name be praised no matter what. Today each of us — one way or another — have a collective responsibility.

CHAPTER 15

Love of Darkness

The Absence of Light

Darkness is a place where light is absent. And wherever there is no light, evil and dangers abound. The devil is the chief of the particular darkness referred to here. It is an imitation, in the sense that God had spoken to the Israelites when they were on their journey to the promised land of Canaan. He used a dark cloud on several occasions but not for destruction but to instruct them and guide them against their enemies.

God actually made the darkness but the devil makes his use of it most, in order to perpetrate evil. Imagine, what the Lord had made—for mankind's rest—is used by the devil and his agents to sow tares amongst wheat! Sin is the order of the day.

109

Majorities whose consciences have failed, have been lured into it. On arrival, they have little or no choice than to succumb and do what is being required of them in there. Very few realise they've chosen the wrong road and when they want to make a change, discover that its a battle and that the correction of error is very hard; hence spiritual warfare.

Evil Members

But the bible says, we wrestle not against flesh and blood, but against principalities and powers in heavenly places (Eph. 6:12). Due to the fear that they just can't fight and the saying goes by humans that, *"if you can't beat them you join them,"* so they end up resigning to giving themselves a rethink and later decide to love it by force, in order for peace to reign. After all, multitudes are on the lane. But they soon forget that the bible says do not join with multitude to sin. Don't be unequally yoked with unbelievers (2 Cor. 6:14).

It also means, don't yield in to what the evil members in your body are telling you to do. Where Paul the apostle said he saw himself doing what he never wanted to do (Rom. 7:18). It is because of the evil members in the body, which were not fully removed.

When you critically view the book of (Matt. 10:36), you will understand what I am talking about. You will agree with me that your troublers are not always human, rather what you ate and carry inside of you.

Many of us have eaten some poisonous foods, even drank in the past, which were projected to worry our destinies, as an arrow of the denier. And at a particular season, it actually springs up to manifest its purposes in us.

Enemies of Progress

It has made us to have bad dreams to the extent, whenever good things are about to happen, which would birth a miracle with testimony, we would be relegated to a failure and disappointment by it; as such it will no longer work out. Let's stop blaming our neighbours that don't even know our stories. Some of us do eat in the dreams. What's in your body is responsible.

They end up finding themselves dining and wining with Satan the devil. What an undesirable association! In the dark places are where most of the heinous crimes are committed, which are against the law of God.

In darkness, they can sleep with somebody's wife, by regarding her for a single girl. That is where most of the evil businesses come from; like the spiritual slave trade, dirty business and spiritual trade. Those in this category automatically become an associate of Satan by embarking on evil missions for the devil, in order to help him accomplish his kind of evil desires. That means, putting people: the innocent loved of God in jeopardy.

Your bad behaviour towards your neighbour could be regarded as darkness here. Some bad elements do like others to cry. They are nothing but a complete obstacle and barrier. Enemies of progress in short, they likely claim to be to their fellow human beings without cause.

We must Examine our own Choices

Darkness can be anything, which has regarded a genuine fellow as a fool in the eyes of their helper. At least, if you are into a business with anybody, you should be able to see the person with whom you are transacting, except on social media. Whereby it has to do with physical contact (in person), if you can't see whom you engage with in the transaction, then please change. I suggest you change business partner, for Christ's sake. You could be killed while your money is also gone.

Men feel benefited most from the dark side of life than the light. That is why if Christ and the devil were to be voted for, you will be very surprised to see how much Satan will carry a number of votes; even more than Jesus the Author and finisher of our faith. Humans are barbaric to some extent only the merciful God can actually help them. Human beings, eat food today which they digest and pass as waste tomorrow. Equally they say one thing and mean another — betraying even their neighbours. May the good Lord deliver us.

Physically we often complain to God that all is not well. Yet fail to examine our wrong choices, which helped lead us into suffering. We will recruit elements: thieves, prostitutes, cheats, murderers, homosexuals, lesbians, heterosexuals, bisexuals, womanisers, mad, stupid, foolish, barren, haters, malice, poor, premature birth, premature death, frustration, reproach, disgrace, embarrassments, and so on, in the dark world and yet complain to God.

"Please, we are in problem helps us." Before you made those choices were you blind? If you don't have the formula why are you bothering yourself solving the problem? You just can't get the answer. It is not a magical issue.

We Reap the what we Sow

Look, how can I choose a style of clothes and having sown it, I'm here complaining about being mocked publicly. You knew that clothes (apart from covering one's nakedness), have the very means of defining a person in the eyes of the public. Likewise, if evil must stop in our human society, every means of recruiting negative elements in the spiritual realm, must be totally cracked down. If not, no way. You don't sow mango and begin to expect to reap corn. It's not possible.

Evil men hated Jesus Christ during his ministry with us on earth because they discovered that He could expose their secretes and that their evil business of cheating would then fail. Yet Jesus died for all to be redeemed for salvation.

Beside the precious atonement made by Jesus, which no man can do, nor in anyway can be repeated ever again even in the nearest future; yet man is still somehow under compulsion or relatively forced until tomorrow, to accept the benefit and then give God His praise, yet feel so reluctant.

CHAPTER 16

Human Compassion

Because the Spirit is in Them

Naturally, some groups of personalities just can't do away with having pity on others because the Spirit is in them. The same thing prompted Jesus to volunteer to sacrifice himself for mankind, for the sake of reconciliation with God. Compassion can bring forgiveness and mercy. Jehovah based His mercy on mankind due to the compassion Jesus exercised on us.

Today, even though, no single believer—by human effort—is yet righteous but when the Lord God sees the atonement of Jesus, He considers them in right standing with Himself. The grace we do not merit (like obedient people), is showered upon us freely because Jesus made atonement.

Today, we all have the golden privilege to approach the Almighty God as our Lord and personal Saviour. Otherwise, who are we to call on God, the Creator of heaven and earth!

As the fall of Adam brought about imperfection of mankind before God, the blood of Jesus (the second Adam) brought about the resolution to the conflict of mankind with God. With the atonement Jesus made, God was able to see something good about man. In fact, from that point, it is a confirmed fact by God that regardless of man's imperfection, something good can still emerge out of mankind, to His glory.

Reach God with a Pleasant Fragrance

In the era before Christ (B.C.), Noah's sacrifice reached God with a pleasant fragrance, which the Lord God so delighted in saying, *"If anything good can come out of man I will not destroy the earth again with a flood"* (Gen. 8:20-21, 9:11).

Today, are human beings really praising and worshipping God? Even during Noah's time, the dispensation of animal sacrifice before Christ, it was confirmed with a covenant by God and sealed with a rainbow after perceiving the aroma of the sacrifice performed by Noah and his family, with a conclusive word that God would never again use water to destroy the earth, as a covenant, which still holds to this day (Gen. 9:11).

A thanksgiving is a praise to God. Therefore to this end, let us love and embrace this endless compassion from God on us through Jesus Christ our Lord; and begin to owe Him nothing but perpetual wondrous praise from the base of our hearts. God receives the melody, for silver and gold belong to Him already. Can you trill God? You must be the type who knows how to praise Him. You must know how to flatter Him also. It is not all about praying to God every time as expressions over necessities. Do sit down and lecture yourself with some innovations on how to please your Creator at least that can enable you to obtain from Him, even what you never expected, trust me.

I Dare you to put a Smile on God's Face

Imagine Him, although superior to your earthly father, knows how to put smile on your father's face. We know He is loaded with our needs but that does not mean we should always send Him messages of requests upon requests, every now and then. I dare you to put a smile on God's face with your beauty, your comedic nature, your stature, your funny nature, etc. You are somebody man keep it up.

Tell God He did not make a mistake by ordaining that you should be formed in your mother's womb, which caused your birth into this enclosure. Come on somebody, just tell God that you are not a reproach to Him, you can't even be one. And that He just can't groan negatively why He made you and that you are ready to do Him proud.

Let your phenomenon attract you with some blessings from God. Remember He is overloaded that no matter your withdrawal of all kinds of blessings, you just can't defraud Him. Do you need happiness? Trill God and tap. Children, money, peace, and all that, please, do trill God in order to tap yours, He is ever ready. You are un-believe-able.

Chapter 17

Humanitarian Love

The Promotion of Human Welfare

This is the kind of love which is concerned with the promotion of human welfare. In it, you can find the acts of sending groups for humanitarian aid. For example, this is what the UN has done for many nations around the world, where they have experienced wars, natural disasters, earth-quakes, floods even pestilence, etc. It is a complete voluntary exercise where the benefactor renders to his beneficiary, without making any demands for payment. It takes God's caring heart to do it without grudge or complaint.

When we talk about humanitarian issues, we must refer to compassion, which is the ultimate. Without love or pity, offers cannot be made nor can any help be rendered. The content also embraces the humane. There is nobody who wants the welfare of another that will not strive to aid the supposed beneficiary.

You cannot be a Messiah to Everybody

Such a one must possess the spirit of selflessness and generosity, benevolence and sympathy, kindness, mercy, goodness etc. Without any of these qualities, any humanitarian aid exercised cannot be well accomplished and the beneficiary won't be satisfied.

You can't expect a receiver of any benefit to be satisfied with help rendered to them with grudges. Would you? It is not possible. If he or she reluctantly accepts, it means the giver or benefactor succeeded only to load the mind of their beneficiaries with enough bitterness that will stay with them until death.

Never force yourself on anybody because both sides will definitely lose. If you do, you do. Let the glory go to God. After all, you cannot be a messiah to everybody, rather you can only be to those with whom the Lord God has allotted to you to meet their needs at a particular point in time. You can even incur problems if you thrust yourself beyond the boundary of your benevolence. Just because you are capable, don't jump to help the wrong type without allowing God to direct you, my friend you will have problems.

If you don't suppose to hospitalise someone and you do, you can have problems and even turn a tenant overnight if care is not taken. The fact that a next neighbour is jobless doesn't mean you should just take him or her to your company because there is a vacancy and introduce him or her to your director. Don't complain if you are fired.

Unless God Sends you - you are Alone

If the Lord God does not send you, you are on your own. Don't be surprised if God allowed it, if that is how you will learn to be wise. If you don't learn in peace you can learn in pieces. Fine! Fine! Fine! It is true that God has blessed you with money. The fact that you are loaded doesn't give you the audacity to go about giving your money to everyone you see, especially when the glory does not go to God.

Why? Well, the simple fact is that, God cannot send you everywhere. Be informed that anything we do where the glory fails to go to God — He can destroy it — being that He is a jealous God. He can never let His glory be diverted.

I know your mind goes to your achievement. Do you think that the glory you obtain from any success goes to you? It is true that you might actually feel it but the Spirit of the Lord God inside of you does take it. And only the Lord God can tell how it is with Him. We humans do not know what glory is; whether it is food or not but God can tell.

If you do business and fail to find out whether God sent you there. I mean, God can't partner with you yet you still experience a flop. It is not possible. If you fail in marriage do a cross-check if He was there. If you err you can only incur punishment as a sign of warning by God not a total failure. God can't fail. Enemies can only fail woefully not God.

Robbing Peter to Pay Paul

There is a course God wants you to study and if you undermine and go for another due to fashion, He will minus Himself and wherever God is minus it is totally baseless. God has instructed in (Matt. 6:33). We can see that God is jealous of number one. If not God nobody else is fit. By strength shall no man prevail (1 Sam. 2:9). This love of God is in everyone it's just that some have been covered. You must pray to unveil and activate your own otherwise you can't really do well.

This love actively embraces eventually everybody in the act. Even the devil is involved, in the sense he still knows how to give; even though his kind embraces with sorrow: give and take. In this context, although the devil owns no property, yet he strives to still and then give to entice even though he is up to something else.

If you hear people saying, *"Robbing Peter to pay Paul,"* this is the source of that idiom. And literally speaking, it means a lot. So, when we talk of giving, the devil is included, as well as the good and bad people alike. It is almost as equivalent as the casual love. Everyone is also involved here. The level of practising and the type one practices, determines one's reputation, nailed.

One can sacrifice a gift just to ensnare. An offer could be projected for allurement. You never can tell, but take notice of gifts that can purge you. This particular love is of diversities. There is the Spirit of love. Some people are naturally born to love. Such people, whatever may happen, do not stop from exercising the true love that they have to the concerned bodies. Evil men just can't change for bad because they are too original to be changed by evil activities.

Orphans & Widows

Somebody can just voluntarily decide to help the orphans. That is charity, out of selflessness, with cheerfulness. Wherever they are they make sure their money gets there, through their postcodes. Even if they do not appear in person, which usually is not compulsory, at least their liquids or substances reach their beneficiaries. The same thing is applicable to the widows whose husbands are gone. When a sailor of a ship is gone, lack of care must set in except the Lord God sends a helper otherwise, the victims suffer.

Women in this condition get assistance from these people with humanitarian passion. They try to show love to the women that all hope is not lost; regardless of the fact that they no longer have husbands. Some of them do adult from the orphanage homes; most especially the kind hearted barren ones, just to cater for as their fosters parents. They do really sponsor the careers of these children from primary to post-primary even up to tertiary institutions.

Besides, they make sure they nurse and give to these children their respective natural education, which is called informal education that they lacked from their biological parents. To the extent that any child brought up through this process does benefit from some good barren parents. Hence he or she can never trace their way back home except they are told and directed. Perhaps, that was why the late Bob

Marley said in one of his albums: *"If you know your history, you will know where you are coming from."*

As for the case of these orphans, they can never know, (and some will not even bother to know), because it just does not serve them again. A tree can be regarded a home in this regard, you know mostly what it's worth to some extent. Some barren parents are equally favoured with children by God, due to how they take a good care of the orphans.

Embittered Seeds Die

Giving has principles, with the seeds that yield the operators a return with blessings. The measure you give out will be surely returned to you. It is a pity that many are bad beneficiaries that hurt their benefactors into having them resigned to a mood, which will kill the seed without any positive yield or return. The meaning of the illustration is that, when you give and you are embittered, the seed of your generosity can die and you will no longer receive any benefits, (*"whatsoever a man sows that shall he reap"*) and that's how the evil ones wants it.

The mistake of beneficiaries is an arrow by the enemy who are either in between them or the beneficiaries themselves, to spoil their seed. They want to kill the interest in the ministry of benevolence. They just want to introduce discouragement and frustrations in the whole process. Some will tell you to pocket what you have and to *"help yourself,"* in order to discourage you in the act. Or similarly they say, *"Keep what you have and let me be."*

Not all Tears are Original

Probably, if it were possible you should reflect your mind back to the point of need and find out that he or she was not truly in need. They were deployed as agents to come and disrupt your acts of chary. You fell victim again because you didn't heed the age old advice, *"look before you leap."* Not all tears are original.

Giving is a blessing both to those who give and to those who receive. Some people artificially go as far as searching for those whom they can render help on a daily basis. At this junction, you must believe me that so many benefactors are not genuine. In this contexts rituals are so rampart. May God help and deliver us.

If the help one is to receive is a sort of help which must carry with a transferring of A's problems to B, it is uncalled for. I advise you, *"don't take it."* If you foresaw a gift being projected this way, either to incurring a problem, I advise you, *"leave it,"* after all you can't die without it. Some even buy gifts to offer people, with a claim to administering to them, in accordance with the will of the true living God.

Inwardly, it is a typically a different thing all together. Giving can occur due to a revelation, which could either be positive or negative. If it is positive, which is from the perspective of the order of the Lord God, it paves way for much blessings. On the contrary, if it is not by God's order (and based on His revelation), it can never work out any positive results and even if it does, it will never last because it is a fake.

Same thing it is with the recipient; if the source of his or her blessing does not connect to Jesus it will never yield any positive result rather it produces problem or negative result.

What's the Real Motive?

Apart from the above charity, somebody could decide to train up a child as a foster parent, which is either by giving him or her assistance, like providing him with a job or education (natural or artificial, informal or formal). This is a similar with the less privileged children, we spoke of earlier, that are very intelligent in our society. They do actually benefit from scholarships by such people with this kind of spirit to help. Any person with this spirit would not mind buying a car for a fellow, building a house, buying all kinds of materials, for anyone who might be a beneficiary of their pregnancy, he wishes to deliver for the people.

Naturally, our Creator made it to be so, that everyone should be a messiah to as many people as are allotted to them by God. The question is with what motive? That is what differentiates good and bad people, with this type of love in the ministry. The logic is that whatsoever a man has that's what he'll give. Thus, when you are offering, always do it with a good motive. Why? Because it humanly reflects on the face. And as such, always position your eyes on the head in order to avoid grudges that can spoil your seed of blessing to others.

Is your Giving Contaminated?

Your beneficiaries may not even bother to collect anything from you or they collect and throw away. He or she does not trust you, to the extent that your gift is contaminated. How? It was your grudges that whispered it to them. Actions speak louder than words. The motives behind your actions reflect on your face and if your beneficiary is aware, they may tell you that they are not interested in your gifts and that they'd rather you put it right back in your pocket and keep it to yourself.

Many at times accept gifts from wrong personalities who rob them of their real blessings. If you are spiritually inclined, you will get to know that some agents of the devil gamble their offerings against the blessings of their victims, whether recipients or beneficiaries. May God deliver us.

Indirectly, people can try and show you some quality of love but when critically analysed behold it was a total fake altogether. Little did you know that they are trying to sit on the side of your happiness. They are either surveying to knowing the sources of your material and financial acquisitions or others. Agents of Satan do come up this way to claiming messiah to any targeted fellow, meanwhile intending to initiate them into his kind of group, where such a fellow can be caged for his or her desirable limitation, if not forever.

Many have ignorantly accepted offers from their fellow human beings. They are in short perplexed in that they just can't explain what they can see and even experience. Today he or she is regretting for not having wised up early; on discovering themselves in an undesirable or unwanted place.

Many are into bad societies due to wrong offers, which were accepted by them out of ignorance. What you accept therefore, could directly or indirectly determine where you are going. A choice can create your part. Make a good choice so that you can live happily. God blesses you.

The Greatest Practice of Love

The greatest of these sets of people that practice this type of love are the ones who will give you their good daughter for marriage, buy a car for you, and even offer you a quality job; open a company for you, build a home for you if you don't have yet so that you and their daughter do not suffer. To such beneficiaries, those parents in-laws are next to God in their lives. Where people use their houses to make money from rent-age, others offer out for free hospitality for the homeless so that they can find a place to lay their heads against sun and rain. Isn't that amazing? Yes it is.

I thank God for whom He is. Despite the efforts of Satan, through his agents, to stop acts of generosity and kill the spirit thereof; God still recruits more and more to boost the moral, including channels to help those in the ministry. Thank You Sir. We are all in awe of You, with endless gratitude.

When you give someone something to use or keep, he or she will turn landlord to some other tenants overnight who can never ask; can you image! Why? They will want you to use your hand to kill the seed thereof. If your compulsion goes out of control, it will now look as if you are fighting even the seed yourself. You must tell it to a few people you know, may be to get relief of the grief saturating your mind, during the process of which you don't know who is whom. Is it that he or she is the last person to come for that thing to borrow to use? Absolutely not. They just want to discourage your tendency to help people, because he knows the importance.

They know if they don't obstruct you and you keep flowing in the ministry, the blessing or the reward of it will explode you in some days, for a greater height. Furthermore it will enlarge your coast. Any good thing you do, which induces you with blessings, I think it is worth doing. Also many people will get to know it and begin to do it. And you know charity brings happiness. As the devil does not like happiness, he attacks it immediately before it gets spread beyond his regulation, where he cannot totally stop it. Honestly, people suffer when no help is forth coming to them.

Used Diabolically against You

Diabolically, when you give a bad person something they must use it against you, believe it or not; because he is not part of those you are supposed to render any help, within your ministry of generosity. Take for example, you offer a sum to someone; it is either he or she takes it as an object from your hand to attack you in return.

You cannot argue it because it is also a ministry to the evil ones. Saying, *"Did I ask you to give me money?"* or *"Have I ever called you, one day from the city or even written you a letter that I am in problem and that I need some financial assistance?"* The fellow might be stressing with certain evil intentions of mind, such as *"Did I tell you my situation is hazardous for me and please mister or misses messiah you must come and rescue me out of my red sea? If I am drowning I know whom to call."*

If you offer crops to them as a farmer, the next harvest season you will nearly die in hunger. If you connect them to your business they flop it for you. If they are employed in your company, they sack you to replace them in their state of unemployment. If you help to rush their sick child to the hospital, they must look for a means to channel afflictions from the spiritual realm into your home or family. What shall we do? Only God has an answer to this.

The advice is that whatever good you are doing pray against the danger involved, because you don't even know who is whom. If you are keeping a date or in courtship with any bad fellow, you are just nothing but a complete goner. Your star, spiritual blessings yet to manifest, your opportunity, your business empire, your investments, your money, your materials are just their target. What a life!

C H A P T E R 18

Love of Giving

Open Doors

This refers to the interest developed in rendering assistance to others. So many are the people whose humanitarian passion is very high. They are so generous that they even go about looking for those that are truly in need, to render their help to, because they know that the Lord God will definitely reward them for it.

Giving is a medicine that heals the wound of those who exercise it on the poor that cry to them for help. It is a gift anyway. It opens more doors because he who gives will receive more and that gives rise to prosperity. If I am not mistaken, that should be one of the principles of giving. As God cannot come down Himself and begin to help people individually, He therefore administers it through His confiding personalities, who will never let Him down.

In this regard, each fellow is useful to each other. One thing is to be errand by God and another thing is to do exactly as sent by Him to do. Until tomorrow God is still looking for faithful people for important errands towards other people of the world. in different lines of ministry. If you are not a genuine messiah, He can never send you any message. Or He sent you and you did not guard it with passion, rather allowed enemies to soil it for you, into doing it for their gratifications.

Due to faces, some people are just afraid to speak what God sent them. They are afraid of rejection by men. They are even ashamed that someone may say they are not eloquent. Truly, some foolish ones may really laugh but does that change the message? I can say no. What matters most is what God sent you for. Although, it is also good to be educated. Paul the apostle went for training for a consecutive three years before doing the work of God. Humanly, your level of education determines the extent you can go, at a particular point in time. You just can't compare a university degree-holder with a primary school certificate.

Giving Spreads Ideas

Humanly, as there's nothing God does that Satan does not imitate, men as unbelievers are also used by Satan to render fake help to people, in order to entice them with some gifts as to induce their attention to be worn into his kingdom. You can see here that it is very possible that a fellow will give without love. But you can't just love without exercising any act of giving to whom you do claim to love.

Giving can spread ideas. Like the lectures received from lecturers in the various institutions of the federal government and others. The knowledge acquired from them during this period of training remains with individuals forever. People do advise others about their experiences in life just to help them derive senses, by example.

Giving can also bridge the gap between the rich and the poor. And that can also make development take place for the benefit of the people, where there is no self centre. It is a sort of weapon to eliminating poverty, to at least average life for the people. Parents are not selfish to marry out their daughters for their true life partners that ask for their hands in marriage.

There you will see some rich ones who will beside that, buy a car for the in-law, build a house and furnish it with all kinds of furniture and electronics for him. On a neutral ground, individuals can do such as buying clothes, shoes, make-up kits, books and other materials and offer as gifts.

In some villages, there are rich homes with electric lights, whose owners may decide to wire homes for the next compound in order for them to enjoy light too. Feeding somebody is an act of giving. Apart from food, you can also give money. Again, you can adult a child from an orphanage home, to cater for them as parents.

There are also cases whereby you have some money but no services. Where there's no one to render you with exactly what you're looking for. And so, as a house maid or a house help, you are giving by helping the rich with things they can't do for themselves. It is just as equivalent as servants serving their masters.

On the other hand, due to our modern era, children are no longer living with their parents but it will come to a time whereby due to age in your parents you could decide in the city to release one of your children for your parents, in order to take care of them by staying with them in order to take up his or her education in the village. A help you render to your relatives is a sort of giving. Jesus Christ gave His life for all.

God the Giver

God created man and gave life for mankind to freely live and enjoy every other form of natural blessings. You were given two hands, two legs, two eyes, two ears etc. in order to be able to do what you must do for yourself, even helping others. Semen is given to man by God in order to reproduce. From what you are given, you can administer to others, in relation to their needs, which is within your power to do. All this is done in such a way that the glory may go to God the Giver.

In a nutshell, there is no useless fellow in this world. God can use anything, to accomplish what He wishes in the life of an individual. Only our Creator can tell who is important and who is not. The distinctions which humans make are totally baseless, unless the Lord sanctions them.

I have often seen people distinguishing between handsomeness and beauty. The question is between, who is handsome and who is beautiful? However nobody is just too handsome, nor too beautiful. Your proportional allotment, as a percentage of beauty by your Creator, determines what you possess at any particular point in time. You can only maintain it then (minus the bleaching of it, or the removal of your first skin, or even the tattooing of it).

Every human is within the six colours of humanity, as allotted by God. And if you deviate, rest assure that there'll be some quarrel to answer God for. I dare somebody to leave his or her colour, as it is naturally. You are unique and nobody is like you. I actually love every nature and originality that the Lord has made of everyone. If you deviate, then it's your cup of tea, but don't call on anyone to share with you (simply because our lives network or as such you would want to rob everybody by collective responsibility). You are unbelievable; God blesses you.

CHAPTER 19

Indirect and Direct Love

Indirect Love

Guys these days do no longer mind the sources of money. One may wonder why guys no longer mind their sources of income; what else if not over inclined with the knowledge of demonic schools of thought. I tell you no matter what it would cost them, all they are after is the money; I mean to just have it at all cost. They no longer mind the cost of supply.

Due to their being over fascinated with it, they run after any of their nearest affluent personalities just to blend with the human standard, with the saying: *"He is trying."* Gradually, little did they know as that one is stretching out his hand in giving to them every now and then, when they are in need of financial assistance, they are heading towards being initiated into bad society — fraternity. If you beg too much to survive, you may end up badly. Try and be self productive to the glory of God. That is why you have two hands.

Some ladies love by pictures. There is a difference between shadow and reality. Likewise, a guy who feels that winning the heart of the parents of his future proposal (by beginning to love her through pictures), is a guarantee for their marriage. Even being over-frequent with them, to him is an act of winning their hearts, as future in-laws to himself.

The Issue is Complex

I encourage you to be particular about the girl in question, in order to know if she is the type that even likes your kind of person, as her future spouse or not. Even though you have to be conscious of yourself as not to go against the will of God or abuse His grace that covers you. You must be informed that there are many different approaches, mentalities and reactions to life, above and beyond courtship or marriage.

You are not going to marry the parents are you? Of course not. If you are therefore aware that the heart of man is hard to deal with, then you must know that you are to go for the girl in question, who has the final say over her life (besides God), else you lose.

Becoming her future husband is not by your human effort and that means you must pass through the normal procedures, for God to help you out. Most ladies decide when they are not ready while some are ready but never decide. The issue is humanly complicated. It will be a very big disappointment if you do not hear from the horse's mouth.

Wrong People - Right Time

There is no amount of frequent visits to her family — on her absence — that can really cut to the base and make you succeed in wooing her for a love into marriage. Some will go to the lady's family and begin to stoop so very low and behave childishly, (even splitting firewood), just because of the lady in question. They want an unqualified credit from the wrong people, at the right time.

Then their name could be called over-humbled, respectful and obedient future son in-law. They will even go as far as connecting parents and friends including friends of the girl's for a way out. If you just cannot toast or speak with the girl direct, forget it. Issues cannot be too strong for the mouth of a man, no matter what.

Craving for money had made many good girls lose their supposed future partners. Just because someone that is a bit well to do has come around the corner to entice and intimidate and so give up their glooming for the good ones. It takes a double grace of God for you to be good in the eyes of a single lady that you propose to, when a fake guy comes around, (who knows how to play his way out).

A play guy operates with a higher degree of competition; though inwardly is a complete fake. *"A lady is just like a flower which is happily enjoying the fan of the feather of a butterfly, not knowing it cannot stay forever."* Uncountable relationships have lost to 419s in this generation and no one can tell of the prospect. May God help us.

Any single lady who can discipline herself in anything regarding money and some enticement, has saved herself from any mistake of spouse. No matter what, God will always direct her. I repeat, *"look before you leap,"* is not fake advice. But they view it as a matter of long process. And again I say, *"slow and steady wins the race."*

Don't be Faster than your own Shadow

Normally, if you are too fast, it is even possible that you must mistake some of your opportunities. Except the King of nature — the Lord God Himself — help you to rewind and correct your errors, you will miss them forever. Even if the opportunities come again, they will not be as they once were, when you missed them the first time around: *"Opportunity comes but once."* Don't be faster than your shadow.

"Iroko is as tall as anything, to the extent a man has to turn his head up to be able to behold the height, yet it is still a part of the materials that help in putting the roof over his head." I don't think a woman can be so over qualified even with piles of degrees such that a man can no longer approach her for a marriage because of fear of too much beauty and reputation.

Going behind it could mean something else. One, you want to use her and dump her; in case there is revenge from any direction, it has to meet someone first before you. Peradventure, such a one might be able to apologise and then that will be the end of the whole matter.

The Beautiful Ones are Stillborn

Two, you can only blame anyone who is in connection to the very beginning of your relationship with somebody. Adam blamed God. If it is a direct issue, you will have to face everything all by yourself. If your mind condemns you that you are not man enough, you can as well seek to go behind the canter. You don't want to write exams and fail, I understand. It is better she says yes or no to your naked eyes; rather talk eyeball to eyeball other than to involve a third party in a case like that whereby you can't tell who is whom.

The beautiful ones are stillborn. Good people are not afraid of failure because if they fail they know where to get up and start it all over again until they achieve their goal. Be happy if you even have opportunity to have experience. The success you can see the victors celebrating today in the entire world, could have you dread of their stories.

Self encouragement is a part of the key. Self consciousness is not left out of the whole system. Please, can you learn to involve Christ in your fish business? Of course, if Christ does not partner with you in your endeavours, you know in this wicked world, in the hand of demonic people, it must be hard on you; no doubt. You saw the case of Peter in the bible. And so, take to be wise. God blesses you.

Direct Love

I personally believe in direct contact as far as love is concerned. When you are interested in a particular lady, go ahead and talk to her first, undermining anything. If she accepts fine, but if the reverse is the case, don't still relent and give up your hope for a search for one; rather go for another. The fact that one rejected you doesn't mean all earth has let loose on your part.

In application for employment, some applicants that are not really sure of their qualifications or the skills needed for the job, are the ones who bother going about looking for a way to pass through black processes. There is nothing like having your ability tested by the management of an organisation, in order to know your credentials and qualifications (even performance), as readiness for the job. It is good that they trust you and know whom they are employing into the company, rather than trying to beat the normal process or laying down procedures.

Fake Lovers be Warned

Many have passed behind the very ladies in question and then end up disappointing their parents in-laws. The fact is that what they could not do to merit their showered blessing on them—which they didn't value—can as well be misused by them and then abuse the kinds of innocent parents who never knew what you concealed at the back of your mind.

Ironically, all they did was to woo their daughter for you; which even with a PhD in the university of love, could not win for yourself. May God deliver you from your treacherous acts. The mug has now graduated and has ended up breaking three people's hearts: The parents and their daughter. Fake lovers be warned.

CHAPTER 20

Love of High Standard of Living

Levels of Comfort

It is an improvement in the human living system. It is the amount of money and the level of comfort a person is able to give him or herself. It is the realization of one's dream. It is the arrival of the level of expectation set by oneself and the attained level in life where one has no reason to worry about many other things. It all depends on how one actually needed it. And more so, how one came up with their plans. This is important.

Apart from the major three basic necessities: Food, house and clothes, this modern era has extended beyond that. To get and enjoy even the basic necessities, requires money. Enjoyment is not itself, when you have nothing to spend as a means of exchange; and that facilitates your living condition to go higher and also determine as to whether it will go down or remain static.

Eventually everybody wants to enjoy life to the fullest, trust me, especially if the opportunity comes their way. When your standard of living improves, you don't count yourself, rather people now count on you. Your outfit, communication and skin must reflect it and that speaks for you too. Look! Let me whisper this briefly to your ears. Time had been created by God, therefore branch from it, split and arrange your own because there is no special time for enjoyment.

Are you Sacrificing your own Future?

If you don't mix your daily activities up with enjoyment, nobody will do it for you. Life has no reserve. It is a pity that majorities do not know this. If you ask them, why don't you eat three times daily? He or she may reply, it is because I do not have time and that he is so very busy making money. If your plan is what takes your chances of taking a very good care of yourself and you always think about the future— what if you die before that future? Then comes the people who did not know how you suffered, with a tendency to eat and enjoy themselves over the results of your sweat. Can you imagine that?

Here comes another question, are you a sacrifice? Or were you born to sacrifice your life for others, at the detriment of your own soul, without any positive care for self? Can't you see even when you try to please your people you can't just please them all, let alone people of the world.

I am not against any act of generosity. Please, get me right. You must try where possible to attain a level of proper improvement for yourself, because life is just too precious to be misused just like that. May the good Lord help us with time issues.

You must Balance the Whole Equation

The big person in town depends on how you enjoy your life. If you are only big for the people, look, your life is questionable, believe me. And you are big for nothing. The advice I am giving you may cost you money but if you systematically follow it up, you will have balanced the whole equation. And there is a tendency that you will give yourself a smile at the end of the day. Since positive achievements are what usually give birth to celebrations.

For instance, you are working as an employee, you must be earning high in a good reliable company like: oil, gas, construction, car, manufacturing, even judge, higher ranking officer, bank manager, pilot, sailor, doctor and engineer, just to mention a few. You can even be a peasant farmer and you still know how to scrimp yourself. It is still okay; in the sense, your level of belonging must determine how you do it. You must be such that know how to minimize your stress and cost but maximize your comfort or profit or relaxation. This is because income determines demand.

Living in a comfortable home — not just a house — is vital, which is either bought or rented with a minimum rentage. There are some workers who earn high and even when government subsidises the cost of productions and thereby reduces the price of things, yet their salaries will never be reduced. I believe as a wealthy personality, you should be able to drive a good car, if not cars.

A Family must be Governed by the Spirit of Jesus Christ

Living conditions do not end by merely ordinary physical wealth or material acquisitions, it goes beyond that. You could be rich and if your family is not happily united, your standard of living is not improved rather it is poor, for your emotion is down man. You can't tell me that you are financially and materially buoyant, when you are therefore enduring living with a nagging woman or a brutal husband, with disobedient children, which is totally uncomfortable.

Happiness is a part of good living. As a married person, the foundation of a good living starts with a good husband or a virtuous wife. Crowned with quality children who obey simple instructions, is a vital expectation of a married couple. Most importantly, it must be a family that the Spirit of Jesus Christ governs, to the glory of God.

Also those who surround you — as people in your zone of residence — they matter so very much in the whole issue. If the kind of people you desired are your neighbours, then you have gotten it right. Some neighbours are spoilers. If you go to work and on your return your wife is giving you attitudes, based on the advice by bad advisers, guess who? Of course; your neighbours. Would you like it?

Run from the Venom of Bad Advice

Some women are like babies that don't know how to keep secretes. Hardly had you entered your home than your woman began harassing you with issues. The good ones do know they are to run from any word of a serpent, which is a venom that can poison her home or marriage. If you therefore, love your marriage run from such advice.

If at all, you were told that your husband is a murderer or even a womaniser, please let him in the house first or at least finish eating. It is not good to overload him when he's just arrived home, from a long work day, and present such strong matters like that and expect the accused to embrace your questionable behaviour. It's not possible, so be reasonable.

A tired man would need peace. A tired person would need a warm embrace. A tired man would need even a peaceful welcome. For some hours he's been away from home for goodness sake. A tired man would need a hug at least to feel like someone. Could you please be considerate for once? Drop your inhumane treatment of him and learn to address him in a good manner.

You should know, culturally we have human conformity. The fact that you are right, does not make you right when you do not present your grievances in the right manner. Assumptions or insinuations can make you beg, even your enemy, if care is not taken.

Carry Light & don't Fear

An accuser must be polite, without which the case may turn to another side of the coin. In presenting or reporting any case, an accuser must follow orders of protocol. I do suppose an accuser must possess characteristics, which will earn him some respect from the supporters of the truth. You must be humbled such that you can be embraced. You must be polite. Learn to stay in your honesty and truthfulness. Don't change your colour, else you are a chameleon and nobody is ready to identify with you. Carry light and don't fear.

The fact that you are in the light does not mean your enemy will kill you. Know quite well that God is original, unquenchable light itself and so it can never die. You can't say you are right and then you begin to vibrate at the top of your voice and then expect someone to talk or judge in favour of you.

If you are right, you must respect your dignity. Except in a situation where one is under compulsion, then it can even be considered another problem entirely, if you blow up. And if care is not taken, your enemy might then even be considered right, even when he is wrong and should apologise to you.

CHAPTER 21

Love of Neighbour

Those with Immediate Proximity

A neighbour is the immediate person that is next to any individual body at a particular point in time. The environment and atmosphere could be anywhere any time and any moment. If someone does not get me right, let me be brief, specific and concise here. The people with whom you live in your house of residence are your first neighbour number one.

Secondly, your co-worker is your neighbour. Your partner in the business circle is your neighbour. Your passenger or your co-passenger is your neighbour aboard on bus, train, ship even on flight. In the court of law and in the police custody, the direct or next person to you is your neighbour. Your fellow prisoner is your neighbour. At the open market,

149

shops and supermarkets every direct or next person to you is your neighbour. The farmers have neighbours. Teachers have neighbours. Students have neighbours. Try and live as you are supposed to with those around you at any particular point in time.

In church, Jesus made it clear to us that as brethren we are direct immediate neighbours to one another (Matt. 12:46-50). The issue about neighbours cannot be over emphasised. Please, get it cleared and hold on to it. And also pray to dwell in the midst of the desirable ones who in turn desire you too.

No One is 100% Self-Sufficient

You see, cooperation and unity are things of worthy practice towards one another and it is a thing of joy when it is well accomplished. It is because we are all useful to one another; that is why we must maintain the relationship of neighbourhood. There is no one in this whole wide world who is completely self-sufficient. You cannot be solely satisfied if your neighbour does not contribute his or her quota to meet your necessities. What you don't have, the other may have it, and so you can easily exchange with each other in the services.

To this end, we can conclude that no single element is useless. You could say, *"Am I an economist or an agricultural?"* But let me tell you, your common advice is expensive to whomever is concerned; let alone food, clothes, connections and true influence. The bible says that the body is more than raiment (Luke 12:23).

It is a thing of joy to co-habit with desirable people, who in-turn like you too. This is the prayer of everybody. There are so many advantages attached to this opportunity. Apart from your intimate relationship, your property is saved. Your secrete are 24 hours intact. And there is no fear as to whether any of them may bewitch your children. The sharing of ideas and planning together are to some extent always common among them; that is after a certain degree of trust and reliability are established.

Mutual Respect

This intimate relationship does not stop there, rather could forward still to induce the concerned with business acumen in the partnership circle. There is usually a trust and confidence because everyone minds his or her business. It lightens a burden due to help they render to one another as a result of sharing problems with one another. What does the bible say about being your brother's keeper? Everyone of them respects each other's policy, hence cleanliness of environment and home, while dealing fairly with one another, these are the order of their days.

If peradventure, it happens that quarrels arise between them, they are quickly and amicably resolved because the likeness is always there. The percentage of tolerance between them can only improve as they gradually get to understand one another. No gossip and no external body comes to settle them.

What can usually make you and your neighbour quarrel? When your neighbour is noted with a tendency to double cross, in order to take undue advantage over you, it is certain of course that you cannot just take it (2 Cor. 2:11). That will take us to the cause of a neighbour's trespass. When a neighbour is inclined with demonic powers, he or she could try the other as an errand by demons. And if those that are targeted can't take it, they both can have problems in their relationship.

Enticed

Powers have done terrible damage to the union between neighbours, more than anyone could possibly think. Neighbours are like teem mates. When anyone allows the order of the enemy to prevail, the result can be negative. I suppose here that a collective responsibility can't be evaded. Please don't be enticed, it can make you perverse. What you crave, can possibly be your weak-point.

If you see more than you possibly can, your encounter may just be allurement. You can also see that the source of one's spiritual insight matters. If the perspective of your spiritual insight is not positive, your performance will be negative. If you are doing something that hurts your neighbour I would rather prefer you leave it. Remember we are expected to glorify God. And so, if what we do at a particular point in time does not give God the glory, we missed it. Who then are we trying to please? If we can't accomplish the ministry of nature as assigned by God (Gen. 1:28) what part are we?

CHAPTER 22

Love of Landlord & Tenant

Fixed Assets

A house is one of the fixed assets, which yields a continued income for a very long time. It could be regarded as a long term investment as an asset to the owner. Due to this fact, almost everybody likes to own a house, if not houses or even an estate or estates, where he or she can put tenants. Besides the money involved, some landlords like to give out their houses for rent to their desirable people. They would like interested persons to rent their houses for the sake of peace and regularity in the payment of rent.

When they have the same spirit, they delight in such tenants and even give room into part of their private lives, such as participating in their celebrities. Basically, such tenants must be very neat and clean.

There are some tenants that even when they have finished building their own homes, they will not leave their landlords, due to the amount of benefits they receive in the house; perhaps free rent, comfort or other.

However, sometimes try and get brief with it when the case turns up this way. Know that there are some other personalities in the queue that want the same benefits and if you over delay your exit, you might just prolong their pains in the situation.

Some landlords can be so jealous that even when you are not at home, they can have the nerve to open your door with their master key, in order to inspect what you keep in the house. To him or her, you are a suspect. If peradventure you incidentally caught them, they will say, *"I am just trying to fix up one or two things in your room."*

Meanwhile, they're very particular about things that they are not too sure of, like whether or not you are a drug addict for example. They might have assumed this for quite some time before attempting to verify it with some evidence.

CHAPTER 23

Business Love

Love of Business Partnerships

This is a business organisation where two or more partners join their heads (ideas) and resources together in order to form a relationship for running a business. The motive is usually for profit. Business is a popular job opportunity for a certain percentage of world inhabitants. Due to the less stress and convenience that it poses, the majority troop in to undertake it. It connects you with people who you can have a share of ideas with.

As a result, some business men and women prefer those that have something to offer. Therefore, if you have nothing to contribute—whether cash or ideas—you are not worthy of being an associate or even a friend.

155

Business is a fast road to success, hence riches and wealth come as a result. Business people are well known to be more than the civil servants. And so, it stimulates pleasure and fun. Some employees prefer to create intimacy with their bosses, for the sake of promotion. Some colleagues become very close friends and then business partners, due to certain complications that can arise in certain lines of work.

Keeping close to a higher business partner would thereby render one with certain possibilities for lectures in order to be able to tackle any related problem. And this could therefore lead to the transferring of knowledge. It brings improvement to whomever is concerned, to develop this method of readiness in order to learn from those at the top. If need be, such a serious person can then decide to branch out on his or her own, for reasons of personal investment.

Greedy Business Partners

Some business partners are very greedy. Greedy in the sense, they just don't satisfy with their dividend no matter what. Instead, they prefer to wish or even give their partners problems in order to have them spend their benefits on worthless issues. Do you know there are people that do not want you to experience any yield back income. They would want you to flex them up with your own by becoming too frequent in your place more than usual. And mostly when you are the type that does not want to be let down with the saying thus: *"He can't afford to offer anyone with a cola nut."*

You may be wrecked if you always strive to impress people, by spending to entertain them, when it's not even necessary. Too much of everything is bad; just seldom is quite okay. But good people can only understand this with you anyway. Some people went and listened to Jesus preaching only because they heard that He fed people. People can troop on you, due to what they assume you can offer them, or can expect to benefit from you. Not because they like you. In fact, you're a nobody when it comes to natural likeness.

Love of Investment

The word investment simply means an act with money, which you do in order to be able to make more money. One can decide to open a venture in which one may not be able to do all the work that's required or the extra labour to do it. On the other hand, it could be small or large scale business, even an investment. The most important thing; is it capable of yielding back any return to the owner.

There are many reasons or purposes for investment. *"An idle mind is a devil's workshop,"* they say. Global governments until tomorrow are working: mentally, physically, mechanically and emotionally on this, in order to resolve the trend of unemployment, which makes the world's youth constitute nuisance in our society.

It is a known fact by both individuals and government that when this particular major problem is successfully taken care of, crime rates are drastically reduced, if not totally alleviated. And you know what that means to the law enforcement agencies? Less work to do. At least they can concentrate on other services that are needed. Governments would be joyous to find formulas to resolving all of their problems.

Pregnant Ideas

Investments are not only meant for governments. The only way it will be easy, is when the major aspects are tackled by the government, in order to encourage individuals to go into investment. One, ideal security must be at least provided with the people over life and property. It is only when there is assurance of this that individuals have the zeal and courage to forge ahead in order to deliver their pregnant ideas.

There are individual bodies who can help the governments of their nations with different establishments, to absorb available unemployment in the country. But individual security is limited.

Light is another very import reason. For example, governments must play their main role well, because the provision of light—to an entire nation—cannot be made except by the government. The amount of capital required to install a constant power supply, all over the place, is too much for any individual body to afford.

The government has to sit tight. We all know what it takes to cater for the masses in every nation. But no matter what, a nation cannot be so poor that her government becomes the automatic epitome of poverty. No, never. That has not been, it will not be, and it will never be.

C H A P T E R 24

Love of Establishment

Long Lasting

It is any organisational set up, with the purpose to render services to humanity. It could be an institute, hotel, research institute and educational establishment. Or any profession with power, influence and authority such as medical, military and political. And anything which has a legal certification to last for a long period of time is known as an establishment.

There is nothing that the government allowed to be established that had no quota or percentage to contribute to her pulse. Therefore, every set up and organisation, is a source of income to the government by tax. It is a part of the economy of any nation. There are some private enterprises with a minimum of two partners, but employees or shareholders of about twenty. And so, it serves as a source of employment to the people.

We all know that some big private (LMT) companies do register with the government. That made them to possess two certificates known as: Article and Memorandum of Association. Due to the fact that they can never allow public scrutiny into their privacy, it now serves as a cover up, for some illegal businesses. Articles of Association make a company be legally recognised by the government and the public in general. While Memorandum of Association covers all internal affairs of the organisation or business.

Collection of Bribes

Some private owners of companies do collect bribes from young applicants before giving them jobs. They also use this same opportunity to enjoy young ladies by demanding that they should pay in kind before employment is made. Even after being employed, they still play with them, anytime they need them, by booking appointments in hotels, in order to have their fun and quiet time together.

There is a mystery here. It all depends on how the company was founded — the foundation or alter on which it was built — otherwise the requirement for sex before employment wouldn't be necessary. Similarly, some ladies who felt that money is love and that are really morally loose, do force even the managing director (MD) to love them by sex. Organisations and Establishment are camouflages for so many atrocities, which you wouldn't believe could happen in this secular world.

In short, the activities could only simply be by the ancient inhabitants of Sodom and Gomorrah. It is in fact not properly ideal to send a wife to work or to clean, if you don't have 100% trust in her. So, as some of us have no choice, well we thank God.

Illegal Businesses

So many are directors and supervisors who run illegal businesses with drug addicts by the privilege of the company. If peradventure they are caught, the influence of the god-father will free them. We have what is called normal partners, that just lend their names for people to run businesses and also to establish organisations, which probably may be fetching them with some homages also with income. Humanly, when one learns to appreciate one's benefactor for his or her umbrella, it can then last long to cover one against rain and sun.

Some directors can decide to travel for months, even across the globe. A particular company can grow big and decide to have branches all over the federation and even beyond. With these, advertisements go round at a fast rate due to its products across the globe. It is a very lucrative source of collateral security for the owner and the company to obtain loans of any huge sum with a minimum interest rate of a long term. The confidence is that the bank has trust in the company, with some guarantee. Also some managing directors serve as guarantors for employees and friends to obtain loans.

Very Few Establishments are of God

So many are the activities of establishments, which are untold. It is only a very few establishments that are of God. Not that it is bad to progress but when you are critically analysed, the sources of thriving for some companies are from the negative side of the spiritual realm. The name of the company can cover up smuggling and human trafficking. So many directors are not pure. Some companies are like a cistern that flows with good and bad waters. If you don't know, you can never know.

In short, work can make you save your time or spend it judiciously due to the allotted opening and closing times of the organisation, you can have some quiet time for yourself afterwards. It helps you to develop your skill. It can lead to a branch of ideas. If you have been long in a particular line of job or business, it is likely that you can discover inventions from there. For example, one of the associates of Leonardo di Vinci found a sketched bicycle diagram even before the inventors many years ago.

When you are a party to the global establishment, you are bound to have so many friends, both known and unknown. Popularity is sure, since people like to identify with wealthy people and notable figures in our society. It earns you great respect from far and wide.

People Seek for the Greener Pastures

The blessings of God come through whatever good you are engaged in doing. Governments and individuals, with the help of solicitors, recover their debts from bad debtors (with the help of companies on a serious bargain) either by amortising or paying at once, either by cheque or direct cash.

The level of establishments in a nation determine her government, company groups and individual solidarity. It attracts increased population, since people must seek for a greener pasture. Also establishments can stimulate development, wherever they are situated. And with the help of tax by the tax payers, governments are covered with some budgets.

Chapter 25

Love of Marketing/Trading

Gains vs. Losses

People who have read about marketing in schools are very happy to undertake almost any job, which has to do with their profession. They are so highly oriented that they're always busy all the time. The disadvantage of businesses run by these people is minimized. They love to exercise their brain when it comes to the practical. They could either be on wholesale or on retail or at a time depend on the business being set up, whether large or on small scale. They ensure that every record is kept, which shows at the end of the month whether they're making gains or losses.

However, in all cases the usual motive for setting up a business is profit. And it has so much advantage when

165

ploughed back profit is made for further expansion of the business, in the nearest future. And if the sole proprietor would like to expand (because not every business person likes expansion), it all depends of the level that he or she belongs in the acumen.

Educated for Business (Shoes have Sizes)

Going large-scale can pose some business fellows with certain fears. One, lack of knowledge to keep records for check and balance. If you haven't the ideal education, you just can't run a business of a higher level. Because you wouldn't be able to tell whether you are even making a gain or a loss.

If you employ, you don't even know whether he or she is cheating on you. Employers may turn employee. God forbid. We can all see that shoes have sizes. I also advise that if as a business person you're making progress; never feel so happy to move for expansion to a level you can't control on the long run. May the good Lord help some of us.

Some that have tried it, are crying today, regretting who sent them. However it is a business, which means either you gain or you lose. But if you are very careful to apply the wisdom and knowledge of business acumen, you can minimize the risk of a total loss. The level you can control and regulate is very much okay, by any good business person. It is less stressful and convenient.

Unrestricted

This is usually more possible when it is a sole trader, as they are not controlled by another person nor must they consult with any boss before deciding what to do at any time or any moment; there are no restrictions. The business could even expand to the point that they employ workers to work with them. It is peaceful, since no one else restricts your doings.

Working as a sole-clerk, requires nothing but your academic qualifications, which determines the level you can start at. Then if you are the lucky type, your credentials can attract you with a quality salary to begin with and for further promotion as time goes on. This may relatively depend on your performance, as well as the level of the fast growing of the business.

Trading is very nice. When you display your wares or products on the shelves according to their strategic orders it attracts customers. And that moves markets to improve rates of turnover.

You must be polite to customers; this makes them patronise you. In case of any misunderstanding, you must try and handle issues amicably for the sake of future business transactions.

Fearless

Remember, nobody is above making mistakes. But at a time, it can as well be corrected. The key to a successful person is the wisdom to recognise when a mistake has been made and have the ability to know how to correct it and forge ahead. He or she must never be afraid of failure. If you are afraid of failure, you have not started.

The most cheapest way to making money is by embarking on petting trade, where there is opportunity, even if you do not have a big capital to start on a large scale as a beginner.

A quick return yield back is embedded in this type of business. The only thing is how did they contribute by tax in order to help the federal government in many things? Well, it all depends on the system of the government of the nation in question. As you can see, that actually determines whether and how they are going to legally operate for good.

CHAPTER 26

Love of Profit

Gross vs. Net

This is money realised from sales, minus expenses. The major motive of any undertaking, which has to do with business, is profit. This profit could either be gross or net profit. Profit is gross immediately you just minus the cost of your purchases, while net profit is after all forms of expenses incurred during transactions, which is usually at the end of an agreed period as programmed according to the business; daily, weekly or monthly, even yearly.

The wise business men and women beat down their prices. And then have their sales increased in order to improve rates of turnover. Maintaining this process can generate much income at the end of the day; hence wealth.

169

Assets can emerge from or by expansion as a result of plough back profit, as that will generate enough money to be able to buy land, buildings or houses and cars, or open other branches. It lightens responsibilities since there is money to take care of things. It takes the patient type, to stay on the level of sales with a very low price. This is because goodness only starts to yield positive pay back after a long period of sacrifice.

Many have because of agility raised the prices of their goods and thereby posed their customers with the stress it takes to actually afford it. If you as a business fellow are saying that you don't want to be left out on the issue of current prices, it is like you are indirectly telling the public that your decisions depend on someone who was not there when you got the idea. May the good Lord save you from His rod in Jesus' name.

Undue Advantage

Profit is not only applicable to business transactions, rather it goes far beyond what anyone can ever think of. For example, acts of judging one another; we all tend to probe whether this or that is trying to take advantage of me. Look, what is really the motive of doing things together? Of course if one is truthful here, it is simply nothing other than profit. Anything that has nothing positive to offer you as a person, isn't worth doing. Nor is it in anyway worthy of embracement or even association.

It is nature. But what I think someone is trying to say is undue advantage, such that we don't really accept as human beings. No one accept even a destroyer. What will kill you, run from it. What will rob you, run from it. What will betray you, run from it. What will ruin you, run from it. What will scatter you, run from it. What will divide you, run from it. What will frustrate you, run from it. What will condemn you, run from it. What will embarrass you, run from it. What will embitter your mind, run from it. What will rubbish your mind, your joy, happiness, your peace, run from it.

Undue Profit

What will make religious your gift by the Lord God, run from it. What will make you lose your good friends, run from it. What will ruin your matrimony, run from it. Run from rash. Run from abomination. Run from any contrary from societal conformity by God. Run from perversions. Seek what the Lord God wants you to do, based on your destiny, as the true purpose of your birth.

This is where you can lay in your grace to operate freely without obstructions. Someone else may want to view it as a crime because they don't know. That is only between you and your Creator. But you will also have to be very careful due to mistakes. If you offend your angel, who is going to defend you? You understand what I am trying to say. Profit is not a bad thing. The only thing is that, if it is undue profit that's when it is questioned to order.

CHAPTER 27

Love of Loss

Trading

This is when the expenses is more than the profit realized at the end of the trading period, which could either be daily, weekly or monthly or even yearly as the case may be. One would begin to wonder how would someone likes to run at a loss in business whereby some are praying to make profit with a huge sum of money. This happens at times when most especially the business in question does not belong to the trader who is directly in operation: who takes the day to day active part in the business activities. It can as well be in a case whereby the owner sold it purposely in the dark world by choosing to be poor for the enrichment of another person.

The sale-clerk may not have interest in the progress of the boss but his salary at the end of the month. So, the attitude of not my father's business could be tagged a complete witchcraft here. This can happen where the sale-clerk does not give a good attention to the customers and that might relatively scare them from patronising the business. When a false record is kept and squander is made to embark on pleasure for fun, such is the result. When the clerk opens late, as well as disrespecting the allotted opening and closing times also, the business can flop.

Wreaking Havoc

He or she can as well embark on the uses of charm, diabolical power, even witchcraft, in order to work against the progress of the boss through the shop. If he or she is not the only one in this plan against the owner of the shop, (serving as a delegate from the witch kingdom to attack and wreak loss on the business of his boss), if care is not taken they could succeed. If alternatively they are short of ideas to bring the boss down they can rather pass through the boy or clerk working for him; provided the mission is accomplished.

Where you are not and you do not belong, no one sends an errand there, be it good or bad. Likewise, when the sole-proprietor is noted with some crime in the past and retaliation is only on this medium. Attack could come on him. Enemies could gang up against his progress. When the progress is mostly found challenging to the oppositions. To this end, everything about him is offensive. Out of jealousness, they could strive to bring him even completely down.

Life is not Static

Enemy of progress can be in any form. Apart from external enemies who do not want the progress of the trader over his or her endeavours, there could also be a situation whereby the proprietor would want to be pitied by people and that is his personal choice. I want to let you know that people can choose to be in a situation in order for people to begin to have pity on them. If you know yourself, you can never stay where situations placed you. Life is not static man, move on. There are better days ahead.

He or she could sell his business over night and at day time begins to flop. We can see here that one man's poison is another man's food or meat. It's just like some elements who plan to kill the sons or daughters of their neighbour, so that they may be bereaved with loss. The reason which might attract that havoc may probably be that the child is very wealthy, intelligent, handsome or beautiful with a bright future.

Evil people like their neighbours to labour in vain or even introduce wasted years into their lives. And that even if you may actually be somebody in the nearest future, it has to be through narrow escape such that you will over sweat above normalcy in that you will have wasted your energy, resources, weeping, murmuring and gnashing of your teeth, so that when enjoying you begin to endure old-age, even with pains at the process. Bob Marley said, *"I am happy, I am sad."* Situations warrants that.

Imagine, life with a blink of an eye someone gets aroused with evil jealousy against his or her neighbour overnight on one or two things, for just no good reason. It takes a car with fuel to go on a journey and arrive at the destination. If you are not bewitched you can hardly do anything to hurt your neighbour. No matter what, something must stir you up without which you can't do anything silly.

People get angry even when no one has offended them physically but you must know that something is responsible for this spiritually. If you kill your boss, what will be your gain? Just that peace of promotion in whatever kingdom you claim to belong. It is a pity.

Stop Befriending Evil Agents

Examine your life if you are not living in a dark world. If you are rational, you should know that we all are useful to one another. Anything wasted is useless. Why do you choose to kill your brother, your sister, your father, your mother, your uncle, your aunty, your in-law, your wife, your husband, your son your daughter?

If you kill your son, who is going to blow debris off your eyes? Remember you are not going to be strong forever. Therefore, who is going to take good care of you? I guess you can see what witchcraft can cause someone? It is not good to dance to the tune of the devil. One day it must dawn such that you will be ashamed as the operator of the whole games. Stop embracing evil allurements. Stop befriending evil agents else, you might soon regret your action.

Who employed you wants the best for you. He could be the messiah the Lord God has sent for curing your sickness of unemployment. Without which you could not help yourself and family. You were crying no job, now that you have gotten one, the devil is using you to rubbish the whole thing. Why?

Why do you choose to embezzle your boss's money and then run for a place you cannot easily be traced?

Or, were you happily enjoying your poverty as a young school leaver without job? I can't understand. You complained of no job. Someone gave you one, you don't want to appreciate. Even though he or she is not asking for a homage but at least do the correct thing in accordance to what brought both of you together in the first place. I believe it was an act of love you were employed by him or her in the first place. Why do you choose to destroy him or her for Christ's sake?

Some have killed their angels, in the form of human beings and yet beginning to look for one. May God deliver you. To this end, may the good God who created heaven and earth punish as many that responsible for unemployment in every federation in one way or the other in Jesus' name (Zech. 3:2).

CHAPTER 28

Love of Cheating

Living a Parasitic Life

In the modern era, this is rampant among the human race. Due to the tendency of making it financially fast without minding the cost of supply but deliberately embark on cheating (419) is actually a global trend. This is the priority of these people just to robe their fellow of their resources in order to enrich themselves at their expense.

If you can't do this, people that show concern about you will immediately regard you an inferior in the human society who do not know the reigning business; while the recalcitrance who live by trick are even embraced and regarded as the intelligent ones because they know how to live a parasitic life.

People ignorantly fall victim by mistakenly run into their hands and thereby have their vehicles of progress attacked by the parasites who feed on others just as worms feed on hosts by living parasitic lives.

Some disgrace to human beings cannot just mind their business. Even though the population of women are more than that of men; yet some people develop cult-throat or even become too jealous on their neighbour's wives. They leave their girlfriends, wives or concubines to attack those of their neighbours just to prove that they are smarter and intelligent here.

Avert the Curse

The reasons for this act are very many. One, either as a calculation to mock the owner. Or there is evil seed in her which they feel could be a dream come through on their sides; in case they are allowed to remain together. Agents of the devil go for their assumed property of their master: evil materials. They have been looking forward to hastening to be rich.

And so, coincidentally with the promises attached to the operation they are done. They have no choice other than to embark on forceful act. It could be that the fellow could not avert the cause of it (curse). On the other hand it could be inheritance, which is already in him or her that he just can't do without cheating on other people. Therefore they pray everyday for the ignorant to fall due to their fantasies so that they can be rich over night.

The fear of old age stimulates the yarning to haste people with its tendencies to be rich. People accept a claim of perpetual suspect over something they don't know anything about. Since denied and a claim of innocent is not enough to justify them, they have no option than to practically do what they have been accused of.

The act of cheating has cost many homes to break-up. It has made many marriages run at a loss. Situations whereby husbands or wives want to prove that she is smarter by going round to cheat on her husband is a total sickness the world society is yet to actually cure. The war that a woman caused is greater than every other war you can ever think of.

It takes a woman for the devil to successfully change the world. Just to balance the equation of cheat on this basis is why the devil also lures the husband to go about befriending small girls here and there. Why? So that as a predator, you won't complain if some others eat up your own. May God deliver us in Jesus' name.

A Lack of Trust

The issue of cheating cannot be over emphasised. A lot is actually embedded in the whole circle. And a lot is happening also that some of us actually do not know. You will give someone some money to build a house for you only to collect the money and dash into the thin air. Where are we going? *"Please, take this sum to give to my dad back home,"* only to return to story of theft: *"I was robbed on the way."* Who was there as a true witness? Nobody can actually tell whether it is a dark story or not. You see, you can't trust some people with the issue of money.

Some elements are fascinated; deeply rooted to the core. To the extent, greediness is their number one character. You can say that again. Do you mean business? Are you sure of what you're actually talking about? Don't forget the natural eyes of the incorruptible judge: Jehovah God, right inside of your spirit.

There is no one that can do anything without his or her spirit. I don't know if there could be around the world. But if I may ask, can you do anything without your spirit? No. That is exactly what I am talking about. *"What about my money?" "What money!"* he or she says. *"Are you kidding?"* I replied. No matter your effort effortlessly put in place in order to get to the truth you're actually looking for. You find out that it is to no avail. You know what? Your money is gone. There is nothing you can do about it. What has happened has happened. The only solution is to summon up courage in order to forge ahead. Life goes on.

He who Falls Twice is the Fool

Many have been caused to cry as a result of this wrong contact with bad people who are not rational and even considerate. Set traps on money which does not belong to the fascinated even when they reincarnate, it will still capture them. May the good Lord deliver them. You have your two hands; then I see no reason why you just can't control the witchcraft responsible for that indulgence. May the good God has mercy on some fathers, mothers, brothers, sisters, uncles, aunties, cousins, nieces, nephews, and all the rest that are actually rooted in this matter.

Some of us are crying. You can't raise alarm, you can't beat, you can't arrest, you can't report to the village elders or even highness, kings, and other royal leaders due to the ties of brotherhood in the family circle. My advice is that what one cannot avoid, at least one has to endure it. May God help you. But remember, he who falls twice is the fool.

CHAPTER 29

Love of Gain & Advantage

Progress

There is no born of element that does not want to progress or breakthrough in everything he or she does. Academically, professionally, financially and otherwise, people like to make it, even fast. The advantage is that it makes anybody who succeeds early to enjoy his or her wealth at the right time. It attracts respect and also makes you to have a family of your own very early.

As you can understand that a single lady can't just follow you when she knows that you can't afford your responsibility on her to some extent. It means before attaining to that level one must be economically productive to some extent. It makes you to have rest early to be able to enjoy the fruit of your labour.

Since your children will grow early to be able to take care of their father's property and wealth, you will now rest while they take care of you. Joy must fill the mind of the any good father in this cycle.

No man that does not like a good quality woman for a wife (the mother of his children). Sometimes, wealth could induce her or even the wrong one. All animals struggle to access where there is food. Even the bible recommends a good woman for a responsible Christian. It is a divine favour to be blessed with a good woman. When you have her, good quality children are also sure of that family in the prospect. A successful marriage with a good family is not far from your portion. And that of course could be one's favour from God a reward for one's good Christianity.

Attracting God's Blessing

Gain can only come to you when you have something doing. It is like running a good business can attract God to bless you. When your business is flourishing, you are already in money. But don't fail to praise the good Lord that has favoured you. Amen.

If God favours you and you are promoted in your working place, you are also bound to be rich and that also depends on how you use your money. If there is a vacancy, I believe you will introduce others as God would direct you because it favours you. The same thing it is when your business is booming, you won't mind employing someone to work with you, which he or she receives payment on due basis or even introduce the fellow to a similar business. More imputes more income. But a good quality record can always enlighten the proprietor to stop at the state of equilibrium; else he or she is to prepare for a diminishing return.

CHAPTER 30

Love of Human Protection

Self Preservation

There are times (all the time), when protection of life and property is mostly needed by the masses from the government of their nations. They will conclude, *"Even if it is only security we can gain from this government before her tenure is over, at least, it is okay."* Human protection could be anything measured to preserve it. Each life is valuable. Diabolical as charms or other man made weapons are the measure of protection by man to the believed personalities based on their religions/ choices. The reason for these necessities are not far from the fact that actions provoke reactions.

That measure of protection one therefore gives to oneself depends on who mentored one. And however it may be, if the Lord God is not involved, it can never work, for a very long time. And that is to tell you that some day, it must expire. If God does not build the house those that labour to build it, labour in vain.

When people see negative opportunities, they will mess you up and yet telling you if care is not taken to your eyes that you just can't do them anything. Due to the grief it poses to impart in you, (based on this boast and intimidation of the opposition), the victim calculates and reacts to satisfy his conscience. Either by poisonous substance through food, drink or injection or the worst of all, ask or recruit someone to help eliminate or cut them completely down spiritually.

May God Deliver Us!

Native doctors have helped series of personalities to do this without being noticed. Assassinations are of different phases in the sense, it can happen through different methods and different processes. May the good God deliver us.

Many have submitted pictures to assassins with a huge sum, in order to help eliminate some fellow they suspected with some challenges or even a threat to their lives. Some use armed robbers to perpetrate their kind of evil act intelligently as they choose to execute it in their own ways. Is it not when they are caught you get to know who sent them? If reverse is the case, no one talks or gets to trace to know them to the sources. Apart from that, many people believe using charms or other measures of calculation to protect themselves against evil attack. Although it might actually work at the beginning but at the long run it fails the owner and battle will increase much more than usual.

A Clear Conscience Fears no Accusations

As a matter of fact, sin could cause this or jealousy. Many who were conscious of the wrong they did against their fellows, go about hiring security to take care of them (probably with guns etc.) and if they are gone, they will not have to come and probe them anymore. If you kill in order to cover up a crime you have double consequences to face in the human curt of law and above all, even with the most high God. With that, they feel they have rest of mind and that their lives are secured. Not knowing that security can sleep off or even collect bribes and before they know it, they are already exposed to any kind of danger. They said: *"When power meets power, power will bow."* These people in question are ordinary people in our society.

May be again they got wealth from a fake source; hence they are not comfortable. If you are pure, then what are you doing with bodyguards? You should move like every other innocent person in our society even on the street. *"A clean conscience fears no accusation."* Let's be realistic. Jesus foresaw this complication with mankind where He instructed us to live peacefully with all men. Treat your neighbour right.

Chapter 31

Love of Prejudice

Disregarding the Rights of Others

This is a particular kind of love which is exercised from one person to another based on race, religion, beliefs and sex etc. In short, he or she could be a racist. So many people prefer girls as companions simply because they are girls and boys just because they are boys, as well. It could be a choice, anyway you just can't judge it. They are not aware that they are missing a lot. Where they suppose to gain from one another, they will not because the intimacy is not there.

For example, someone you do not relate with, how can you just awake to go and be asking him or her for a favour or help overnight? Imagine, passing someone by without even a word of greeting all of a sudden you just start asking him

193

or her for a help. Can that work. Check it out. Some of us in that shoe cannot even bother to reply because to them it isn't worth it. It is not possible. And I do believe it is difficult because you are shy. *"Charity begins at home,"* they say. So, when it happens like that, you see that your manifestation reflects your culture.

God has a Reason for your Colour

If you were not born and brought up in the midst of boys and girls, it is hard to blend with the system publicly. To relate with an opposite sex will be so very hard on you. Some of us are so very shy to the extent we would want to disappear on seeing girls. They will feel so inferior even as a nobody. Look, if you underrate yourself, you are just doing nothing but embarrassing your Sovereign Lord. And may He deliver you. God has a reason why you are black. He has a reason why you are white. He also got the reason why you are yellow, chocolate, red, a human being; etc.

Another factor can also be responsible which is not very common; if at all, not everybody may know it. Spiritually, demonic powers can make someone to be very shy of themselves before people without even a cause. When you are over shy, you can stoop so very low (below normalcy). You can begin to stupefy yourself if care is not taken.

When you are shy, you can begin to abuse even your own personality without knowing it. You can be forced to offer what you weren't supposed to, under normal circumstances. You can turn yourself into a slave or fool to your kind of calibre of person without your normal senses. It is an arrow with a syndrome, specifically projected by enemies in order to battle their targeted victims. But thank the Lord God for His word, which says: *"No weapon fashioned against you shall prosper"* (Isa. 54:17).

Shyness is the father of an inferiority complex. Being over shy is a problem even if you are able. It will first of all pose you with the Red Sea to swim even before thinking of what to do. You are interested in a lady as a guy for instance, and you can't express your feelings affectionately, yet certain feelings grips your mind in order to stop you from making a step forward for an approach towards your concerned opposite sex you tend to express your feelings; yet you are restricted from within that you just can't do it. Oh man! You can say that again. An experienced fellow is already aware of this fact.

A Brother of Pretention

Prejudice can make you indulge in it if you allow it. Anything with advantage also has disadvantage. It could also sometimes help you to avert dangers. It is a brother of pretension. It could cause war like religion; since you could even be hostile, due to certain beliefs you also practice as your religion. More than half of your characteristics are bound to embrace some atom of irony to people's impression even you are personally aware of this. If you are a leader, there is no doubt if you will produce the bad type or one. Insecurity must become the order of your days due to corruption no doubt. Your subjects may not trust you. People practising this kind of love are gossipers and are complete liars; their doings are full of eye-service. Only you and God will know what you are up to.

Chapter 32

Love of Sycophancy

Abnormal Flattery

These are people who so much believe in praising others (abnormally), which could be a calculation to obtaining from them. Ironically, the praise is of dissimulation in the sense, it does not directly mean what it says and does. It is just being displayed in order to manipulate you. And if you are not careful, you get carried away and be victimised. It leads to gossip and blackmailing others, which is not good in the sight of God.

All is just to gain ground in order to get one or two things from the rich or targeted person in question. At times, if he or she is short of info, he looks for at all costs in order to be able to fill in the gap of info recorded just to be able to visit the rich that can entertain and welcome him or her in a special way with desirable offer.

Just because the chief or a king or even a queen in a kingdom will offer a cola-nut and a cup of drink, some people can go as far as any length to gather info to relate to the king, which in most cases may likely not be true. Such people believe in running along with others who can only render help to them. Nay! But they forgot that it leads to gossiping others. And it can also run others down completely. The fact that you want to gain advantage from somebody does not always mean presenting info you are not too sure of being correct in order to gain ground at a particular point in time.

The Gossiper is Coming

More also it can even make you becoming much talkative before your audience. Don't you see if care is not taken you might just end up nicknamed, *"The gossiper is coming."* Are you happy over that? Or are you in anyway joyous in bearing that name? In most cases you are named after your profession; this is human nature for you.

A stir can always cause division. And if a stir can cause any atom of division, then a stirrer is a divisional. When all this is known by people that you are responsible, that can automatically debase your dignity and personality even before the concerned body. And you know a good name is rather to be chosen even than a great riches. If it is not important, the bible would not recommend it.

Watering the Ground

Many people have taken this as their profession. How? In some cases whereby certain crimes are very difficult to do without being caught, they apply this method as a key to having their way with it. It is the same tactics used by the same crime indulgence as dubious fellows are actually afraid to embark on their business crimes freely, they resign to gossiping to their neighbours, so as to be able to operate with the guarantee of relating info for the intention of covering up as an umbrella for their indulgence.

To gain backbone for a boldness to embark on naughty business, people forcefully do this in order to water some grounds. May God deliver them. That is why Paul the apostle said: *"You that said don't steel, do you yourself steel?" (Rom. 2:21)* We all know that to be arbitrary is common with humans.

Some chiefs in a king's cabinet do gossip sometimes due to jealousy over position. In the kingdom circle, there are various reasons for this by the so called chiefs, for example as an opportunity to drink and eat cola-nut in the palace and to be loved mostly by the king. To obtain promotion or be favoured in a most special way and many more by the monarch. They can easily cause a misunderstanding and quarrel among people and thereby spoil leadership in the minds of the subjects. May God deliver them, Who doesn't joke with any leadership position. Injustice and perversion can ruin a whole kingdom but remember there is going to be accountability.

For instance a man was helping the only rich person in a village in search for a life partner. Having found one, behold, she happened to be the only daughter of the king of the place. Meanwhile, she was already matured to be given out for marriage. The parents had been so worried about her being still single. They called her one day and said, *"Daughter, you are not getting any younger. So, we are looking forward to seeing that you present to us a man that will be your husband. Perhaps, that reminds us, there was an international business man who came to seek for your hand in marriage,"* said the king and the queen, thinking their daughter would gladly accept and embrace it. Instead, she turned it down.

A Yardstick Measure

The both parents tried different ways, behold, all was to no avail. None of those interested the daughter nor did she embrace the info either. The daughter then said to the father, *"I don't like him."* She further said that she was looking forward to a husband would make her happy. One day, the girl brought a humanly regarded pauper to the father so that he could give her his marriage blessings.

"Papa, this is my husband, I have made my choice," she said. Bless us so that we may go and live our marriage lives in bliss. The parents refused and got angry including the proposal: the rich man for her by the parents. The only recognised rich man in the village who has gone overseas and traded with white people. As if that was the complete yardstick measure to judging a choice of a true life partner for future matrimonial couples to be. He was only being introduced to her by the parents and as a witness.

"Why are you against my choice," the girl said. It's seems you people are not after my happiness. I want to marry a

man who would give me joy. I want to marry to a man who would genuinely spend the rest of his life with me without complaining that I am a burden to him. The rich man thought that a true love was all about money who boldly came around to watch. Behold, he was totally disappointed. Who went away soliloquising at the end of the day.

"Now I know who is dragging this girl with me," said the rich man. *"I will deal with him: I will deal with this boy. I will show him that I am the one-eye in this village. The only black man that has traded with the white people,"* the man said and went away.

Are You a Professional Gossiper?

The intermediary was always looking forward to lying against this poor man in question, whom the girl was in love with, just to defend the rich man and gain ground before the king. As the introducer was about to tap palm-wine as usual, behold he saw the poor man naked trying to have his bath, but no manhood. Note, this is a lesson. If you are a professional gossiper, at times learn to keep certain secretes to yourself. The news you carry could change and you would be backfired. He went straight to tell the only rich man and both of them related everything to the king and his wife. And that got the king more infuriated.

The king's order, which no man, not even the king himself can change; we all know as a royal leader. Emphatically, the king asked the traitor whether he was sure? The traitor answered yes without impulsive. Furthermore, the king asked and said if he got to find out what the man told him was not true, what he — the king should do to him? The man by himself replied and said his life could be taken by the king.

After the poor man had paid and performed all the necessary sacrifices it took to retrieve his manhood, he finally got it back: his manhood. So, the life of the traitor was actually taken, as he earlier swore by himself before the king.

Lies cause Division

Lies can cause division and even death; just as what happens to the intermediary. It can debase and devalue personality; when the person to whom you always relate info (usually not true), now gets to know that you are a fake and no longer trust you. You could still expose them to the public, if you have the opportunity. You know that kind of thing. And they have to act fast in order to stop your coming to them, else they might regret it at the long run.

Some daughters of well to do parents have been impregnated through this process; whose vehicles of ambition and careers were stopped on the high way, by fake people. I bet you, they just don't have any other business, which interests them rather than to go about and then begin to commit all kinds of atrocities.

Respect

Don't respect anybody because you are expecting something from them; rather, do it because it is worth doing. Take it as a thing of nature, which also has to do with culture and tradition of the people to the glory of God. God made culture but man practices it. Therefore, if the practice is wrong, the result it gives to the people will also be wrong. If my reason of respecting you is because I want help from you, it means I am a fool and I don't know what respect is all about. You could have so much tendency to practice it in a good way and all the while the interference as recipients that do not know the value could also rise to abuse it. They misunderstand your intension. One can even quote you wrong with wrong assumption into thinking you for something else.

Discouragement is human and it is an attack to anything good. Where do they think they are going with all these greetings and anxiety? It is only a complete fool that concludes the way he or she thinks to be the mind set of another person when it comes to respect. Whereby he or she has no idea about whatsoever you carry right inside of you as a person. Assumption at times could be sickness to whom does not control it so well before acting accordingly.

Many good fellows have tried their best to dignify others exactly as it ought to be but nay shattered by talk, provocative words and actions even reactions of others who do not actually understand value, but only harbour assumptions and insinuations right inside of them against you just to ruin the whole thing. Even though it may only be done indirectly, it hurts badly. Bad people use it to indulge in so many crimes like: burglars, rape and even gossip.

Wrong Insinuations

On the similar case, some ungrateful elements do sometimes consider your respect to them as a kind of sycophancy or even a kind of sheepishness. Thinking you are just respecting them because you wanted help from them. Or they may even call you a gold digger. Not knowing that, their insinuation is never true. It is rather just a matter of formality by the bad ones. It's just that, it is a fundamental kind of ancient practice which is 50/50. *"If peradventure, one refuses my greeting, one has not done me any wrong."* After all, you can take it as choice not to greet anybody. No one will sue you in a court of law or have any authorization to question you to order.

Everybody is not actually the same; in the sense, greeting does not mean you are poor, rather you reciprocated and forgot that humanity, which always whispers to you that greetings mean that somebody needs help from you. Somebody will ever be helped by those that are concerned as God sent and so, don't let that bother your mind. With you or without you, the ministry of generosity goes on. Simply take greetings to be greetings and help to be help. They are two different things all together; in the sense, you cannot muddle them together.

Wrong environments can corrupt you and even have a negative kind of influence on you such that you now become a donor by transferring the same to those that value respect. And that is if you are not the type who can distinguish between bad and good influence. As you are now being aroused to dance according to their taste and way of life (by refusing to greeting eventually everybody who is due), correction on error is then omitted here.

Misinterpreted Generosity

I tell you the same is applicable to goodness and generosity. Your humanitarian passion could be so high that you would want to offer your last clothes on your back; yet someone is fully ready to abuse it. *"Look at the nonsense they gave to me."* Or *"They just want to tell me that they are materially loaded!"* whereas you never did. Your mind is cleared. You are not even doing it to earn any respect from anybody, as assumed by the so called wrong people to your ministry. To others, who do not understand your gift of nature will also insinuate by going about blowing the trumpet of scandal, that you are trying to use what you have to get what you want, (just to tell the public that you are too loaded) that is the meaning of the generosity you just displayed towards them.

"Actually, the act of generosity cannot be over emphasised," said Clovis. *"Do you know I gave a boy like me a pair of jeans, all I could hear the younger brother say to him was he is looking for a girlfriend from our sisters, be wise, open your eyes brother can't you see,"* he said. Not knowing that wasn't my motive. It is really humiliating with some incompetent fools who do not know the value of a coin. If not for God, help would have no value at all. When you ruminate or rather speculate out of a 100% good being done is usually paid back with 80% negative.

And it takes the grace of God to continue in the act of doing any good even with or without casualty.

CHAPTER 33

Love of Gossip and Lies

Spreading Rumours & Creating Scandal

The love of gossip is an act of presenting others negatively to individuals, groups and the public, usually in an unpleasant manner. The processes could be through stories, talks, or information you have no full accurate knowledge. It is the act of spreading rumours. Majorities of the info disseminated are usually lies. In most cases, the stories presented by them are not usually true. When critically analysed the basic foundation you get is to understand that it is not their fault. Some are cursed by or with it which they needed deliverance. Why, it serves as sacrifice over one or two things to others.

A certificate is a legal paper that one presented with, which certifies that one is actually a professional of what one

207

claims. A certificate is a ticket, which some people present in order to have their free chance to do any bad business they desire to undertake. It is their boldness and confidence without fear of otherwise questions or a reaction to their act. Some police get promotion through informers.

Dubious Characters

These gossipers relate and re-relate what others did (or didn't do) in order to have their way freely concerning illegal business and even receive payment and other benefits. But the end is destruction. Any wealth achieved like that can always dwindle away, as though it has wings, yet the possessors will be punished. Who loses? Of course, the one living dubiously. And that is why you must take to be wise. A parasitic life does not pay with positive results, rather it's under laid with negative pay-backs. You have extorted people unduly in order to enrich yourself.

The highest rumour spreaders are agents of Satan. How do they do all this? In the spiritual realm, it is a career mission to the assigned powers, to inform personalities. Some act as swift locus whose legs are very long, which enable them to actually jump and act at a fast rate even ahead of their victims in order to outsmart them. Don't you sometimes wonder why is it that even before you get to where you are going, it would seem as if someone has gotten there before you and exchanged words with whom you want to talk to before your arrival?

To the doers, it is a recruit on them that they actually needed to dance to the tune. Except God deliver and help them they are in commotion due to compulsion from the kingdom authority there. If you are doing anything mostly negative, don't forget the law of diminishing return.

The question is, *"Is it good that we pity the evil doers?"* The simple answer is based on what the Spirit of the Lord God directs you to do in accordance to the Word according to His will and purpose for everything under the sun. Let's take a look at the case of Pharaoh as a case study. Brother Moses did not say, *"Ah, I got the authority from God already, therefore, I can use it as I like."* Nay, instead, he simply waited for God's order before acted.

Otherwise, if he had prayed for the Lord to bless Pharaoh as rightly demanded, even though, God might not grant it, yet he would be punished for it; for misusing the authority vested on him by the Almighty God. Upon Pharaoh begging for him to entreat God, he ignored (Ex. 12:29). Every action or reaction you display at each point in time, would determine the limit of the order placed on you by the most high God, the supreme authority; else, it can cause redundancy and even punishment.

The Love of Lies

This is an act of saying or writing something about somebody, which in the real sense is not true. It is a mother of scandal and libel. Lies are a complete profession to the concerned personalities or bodies. They do it to the extent and even receive salaries sometimes. It is a black-mail by one bad fellow against the other, which is either being asked to help do it or of a personal voluntary decision to do it all by oneself. It could be a retaliation for an offence committed against one in the past. Some people are very good at this. In that they could credit their phones just to burn in calling for a settlement.

An Idle Mind is the Devil's Workshop

Too much conversation on phone can birth a gossip that one will be summoned for a settlement; trust me. The idea of staying on the phone quite longer more than normal is a clear indication that you just don't have anything doing. An idle mind is truly the devil's workshop. God, please, deliver someone. Have you ever opened your phone during the day time, whereby you are not sleeping only to discover that you missed calls due to a lot of engagements you were actually busy doing? That is exactly what I am talking about.

Idleness caused king David adultery in the bible. Until tomorrow, there are lots of reports about people having affairs with other people's wives are still being made. And when you actually trace the cause you find out that the actor is jobless or even lazy to the core. Too much empty opportunity is a factor which can also birth this insult. *"Be busy till I come."* Is not only applicable to evangelism by the Christians, rather to other things as well.

Please, if your laziness can put you in trouble, treat it. Treat that syndrome before it disgraces you. What can make you attempt to rape, deliver yourself. Take care of it. It may be your sickness. Merely seeing you, one would think that you are quite a responsible person who is worthy of respect, not knowing that you have a sickness. A same image and likeness with God can't just be a fool for Christ's sake. Let's behave ourselves. Life is worth living. Let's be human for Christ's sake. If it is a lie that can put food on your table, you will soon die in hunger because God doesn't joke with lies. Lies can get you killed before even the truth is verified.

CHAPTER 34

Love of Trilling and Flattering

Lavishing Excessive Praise

Trilling is any performance displayed usually for an entertainment which could either be private or public. Apart from that, one can decide to trip and chill with people in order to be funny and make them happy. He that waters must be watered. The day you entertain people you entertain even yourself also. That is even the more reason why you must try to be nice and good to people; so that when it yields a return pay back, you won't cry; the result definitely will be positive.

The comedians are typical examples but the difference is that their case is payable. Individuals to some extent are a trill to whomever is concerned. If you have ever made someone laugh positively, since birth, you are a party to this.

God blesses you. Praise be to God. It is of two ways anyway. Two ways in the sense, it is either you make someone cry or laugh for good or for bad. In the demonic kingdom, they can make you begin to laugh unnecessarily even laugh at people so as to induce yourself with trouble. While flattering is to lavish praise excessively on someone either for good, bad or otherwise.

Flattered before the People

King Darius was flattered before the people by the accusers of brother Daniel; after which they presented to him the main reason why they came (Dan. 6:6-14). They got him committed before telling him the real reason why they came just to have him fall rash before any other thing. They knew quite well that Daniel and king Darius had a tie of friendship.

Praise is something else. You could be praised and then you begin to encounter more trials and temptations than ever or you praise someone and he or she is landed in trouble. Group of women composed a song in praise of David because he killed Goliath. From that day, instability set in the life of David. King Saul began to see him as a threat to his life. King Saul began to search for him under the broken bottles to kill. David was under a spear for years. The battle lasted for many years until the whole storm was over (2 Sam. 3:1). Praised be to God Who saved David from the hand of king Saul. Uncontrollable praise can stir up terrors of enemies around one if care is not taken.

A king who was absorbing the melody of David's music became a sudden terror against David. He became infuriated over any little good David did which when he used to do was giving a melody to his soul. He suddenly got the impression that something was very wrong with David due to what king Saul had at the back of his mind against him. Someone God was using to deliver you from the torment of evil spirits, you suddenly began to seek an opportunity to kill. May God deliver you.

Under the Broken Bottles

He desperately sought for David under the broken bottles to crush. But God so kind who protected David against the king's evil plot. To the extent, he forcefully or cunningly made himself a father in-law to David to secretly and intelligently kill David; as God would have it, it was to no avail. That was a felony of king Saul but God refused to sanction it; so he failed.

His first attempt failed. The second chance got the whole secrete escalated of him by his supposed confiding daughter: a targeted weaponry to ensnaring David. The Word of the Lord which says in Psalm 105:15, *"Touch not my anointed and do my prophet no harm,"* got itself manifested in favour of David immediately. She later remained in the home of David a barren woman all her life as a wife of David. God decides whether evil should remain what it is or allowing to birth anything or be totally wiped off.

There is no way on earth that bad "melons can accompany the good ones in making the soup," never. It has not been, it will not be and it will never be in Jesus' name otherwise, God is not God. And where is the West-wind and East-wind of the Lord of Elijah, which God uses in sifting? He has used it against the locusts eating the vegetation and fruits of the trees of the land of Egypt which were the symbol of their blessings and economic standard as at then to the sea where they got drown to death (Ex. 10:14-19). And that can mean the end of someone's empty pockets, hardships, extravagant spending, rising and falling, labouring in vain and all that.

The Example of Job

Job was another example so crucial in this matter. He was on his own; enjoying all the blessings of God in his life with families: wife and children. As Satan brought accusation against job to the Lord God. In (Job 1:3), as God instead was praising Job, Satan became surprised; he then sought for a permission from God to tempt Job in order to destroy him. As God would have it, He only gave Satan the permission to tempt and destroy his property but not his life. God is good. His name is Kindness in (Ps. 91:14).

In most cases, the flattering must embrace an otherwise called such as a nickname. And so, whenever the voice calls, he or she will immediately switched into displaying in accordance to the name; in order to suiting the expectation why that name was given in the first place. Flattering is also a stirring whisper or hailing in order to ginger up one for excellent performance. It could be an introduction of a king by who bears to him the sceptre as the chief speaker to his cabinet.

For instance, your highness, the elephant who has single handedly uprooted an Iroko tree; the motor of every traditional belief of your subjects. Your will is the subject of your servants. We your people honour you. May your days belong. And may you reign longer than your forefathers. Such are the kings appellations by the concerned body.

One can be flattered to join an armed robber. You can lose your virginity due to flattery. You can as well be flattered to embark on (self called) into a fake pastoral work with a claim that you got a call from the Lord God. It can give you a shoe of lawlessness and you become even a lawbreaker. It can cause any divorce if care is not taken. Find out the causes of an already broken home, you will discover that the one with an evil tongue actually dropped a word of flattery.

A Venom against Matrimony

"Oh mamma! You can be worth a whole lot of money. Just look at you. My friend come out of the egg-shell and make money for yourself. I promise you if you hearken to my kind of advice, under one year, you are already a millionaire. You will be swimming in money. Guard your loin and set your pace on this matter. You will remember me. God punish poverty. As gorgeous as you are, I pronounce you a hotcake of the world, ever of our time. And do you know what that means? Someone will begin to rush you like tom-tom. Give me a file, a millionaire hotcake. A word is enough for the wise." This agent has succeeded in dropping a word of the serpent, which is a venom against matrimony.

Any word is evangelism of its own after being said or released. Having left, the mind will begin to rigmarole over what it has received for real. That will gradually birth a graduate of prostitution later in the prospect. Whether married before or not, that is the end; that was then; a total forgotten issue. The people could also serve as flatter to the villager respectively.

Similarly, Cervi, the son of the soil who does not evade confidential steps of the enemies; you are welcome. Such is a welcome to a rich son by the people of a community, quarter or clown members. After all is said and done, Ruddy who never budgeted for a banquet will organise one by force just to satisfy someone for peace to reign. *"The night landlord is quite different from that of the day."* They can't just hail you for nothing. To at least water their mouth back in place of already used saliva for his welcome by them. Many have incurred debts as a result of this.

Generosity is not Stupidity

You will receive a salary only for your friend to lure you out for a flex, behold on arrival only to be disappointed that you are the one to pay for the expenses. But what about you? If you bargained for an outing and the supposed personality is not the one who paid at the end of the day, it is a complete cheating all together consider that. Come and let's rent a house and pay together and at the end of the day only one of them will be paying; is a cheat. Please, if you are that type, repent, it will get you no where. Nobody is a fool. Generosity is not stupidity. Remember, people were recruited even before you. If the case should change for a better at your turn I think it should be something good and worth embracing. Of course yes. Please repent we are all humans.

There are most people this actually work for. And it induces power for them to really do their best of all. A night of a thousand laughs was a popular example of this trilling of a thing. Some people are really sorrowful and such people needed who can make them laugh and forget their sorrow. Those you often see on television, social media paying gate fee in order to listen to a joke and be happy are not all financially buoyant; it just that they need it , that's all.

Observationally

Observationally, when you can laugh and smile every good time, there is every tendency that you will always appear physically young as a person. Also try to take a look at people who are always fond of wearing long faces, squeezing of noses, murmuring of lips and blinking of eyes as signs to making a negative whisper, you will definitely see that the difference is cleared of what I am talking about.

In all kinds of sports, audience or public expects the participants to highly impress them with a good outcome result. For instance, musicians must endeavour to produce an excellent album each time. And that of course will also make them sell higher. More also in action on stage, he or she is expected to add more effort in order to colourise the stage by the audience. Some people do not only dance to forget their sorrow but rather to also trill the audience.

So many girls can boldly confess that they are only interested in guys that know how to tell them sweet words and who can pet and flatter them. Even if you spend millions and you cannot do none of those things, you are just a nobody to them. This is what easily turns their brain for a love. Furthermore, Kate, a 19 year old girl whom was interviewed on the kind of guy she would prefer. *"I would personally prefer a guy that will always baby me and even add some colourful words and if possible calling me a pet name. That makes me actually feel at home and incline that I am a part of his priority."*

"A matured girl or a lady should be able to know whether she is a friend-with-benefits, a girlfriend or a fiancée. I just like being flattered by my real guy, not only let us play every time. Sometimes, you know, even though it takes you to catch some fun and relax yourself; chat in a quiet cool place. At times, you stroll out to feel each other in the act by casually played. Taking some stroll and do a kind of window shopping is interesting," concluded Kate. Rose, 18 years old girl said something that interests me. *"Based on what my friend has just said, anything more than that doesn't strike me into freaking and you know that kind thing; I beg your pardon."* *"Please, spare me of this so called old-school dating and frequent bed-play. I would rather prefer we change the subject,"* said Titi; a 19 year old girl.

Truly speaking, trilling stimulates a kind of closeness which can generate even urge for an action. I believe you get my saying. It helps mostly those who have over rocked their lives such that they have no regard for sex that much. In any relationship between opposite sexes, trilling and flattering are so very much important. And that depends as to whether or not the relationship will last. In this, material things and finances do not count by any lady that deserves petting words, trilling and flattering; above all attention of her date around her which is worth more than a million and is much more than anything else.

Flatter the Dog!

That reminds me, it's just like a hunter and his dog who usually goes out to hunt game or animals for sales and a consumption. Therefore, if the hunter must kill as many animals as possible, it depends on how he is able to flatter the dog in order to ginger up the dog to make it run fast and active in the bush for the business for the day. Sure! You find out that even if the hunter is holding a gun and he does not shout and roar his gun is useless. And they won't be able to realise anything at the end of the day.

The same thing is applicable to juju and its chief priest. You see, he must learn some incantation to always say in order to flatter the deity, which he acclaimed in that it can help him to do some jobs he actually wanted it to do. Diviners aren't left out of this same issue. For instance, before even anything, he or she does not always forget to pour out libations including some chewed alligator-pepper for a total sanctification. All these together enhance the concerned spirits to reveal every secrete he or she needs to know by the problem at a particular point in time. The brotherhood and fraternity believing in the act of invoking the evil spirit guiding their coming together as one in order to instruct them of what they must do. And the responds would determine as to whether it necessitates ritual or not.

CHAPTER 35

Treacherous Love

Trickery

This is based on what someone higher than you does in number and can obtain without you knowing it. They trick you like 419. It does not matter where it comes. The most important thing is that you are aware that it exists. Brother could do it against brother or sister against sister; the same thing is applicable to sisters on brothers also. He or she could pretend to you but meanwhile seeking for an opportunity to harm you.

This kind of love is common mostly in a fake relationship. People on evil mission can condescend to exercise this love over their target; provided they succeed. The mission could be on personal vengeance for an else fellow by money or others. Assassins use this method in order to do a clean job of elimination of any targeted soul without being caught. The reason could be that the fellow in question is scarce and so there is no alternative than through this means.

It Takes Corn to Capture a Fowl

It is either they involve a clean beautiful girl to help them harm him or her by carefully poisoned him to death or intelligently bring him to a quiet lonely place where he or she could possibly be killed without being noticed. That is felony. It takes corn to capture a fowl.

This evil kind of love comes from the heart of man. This is because, whatever anybody wants to do, he or she must first of all think of it in the mind before even following it up with action. This love works by all treacherous means like fake help in order to convey the intention to another bad thing. It can as well be regarded as an allurement. Cain used this method on Abel his brother due to uncontrollable anger of evil jealousness (Gen. 4:8).

Occult Practices

It can bring in bad ideas to flop your business. A treacherous friend can easily trick you to where you will lose your virginity like them, which you might likely have vowed to God as sacred to His glory over your life. It can make a so called friend even a biological brother or sister to lure you into occultism. And you know occult practices are a dangerous game against the life of mankind.

You could be forced when you are already in it to join any corresponding group you are suited which may likely be armed-robbery. Think of what will happen to you when you are caught by the law enforcement agents? You can be condemned by the chief of justice with death sentence.

The question is how do we know a treacherous lover? *"By their fruits we shall know them,"* even though it's never written on their foreheads. Someone should please be careful so that before they reap what they sowed, he or she does not become their prey. Evil doers will see clearly that it is about to catch up with them by nemesis as a result they will begin to seek for who to make prey once and for all. This time around, if you are victimised, you can't imagine how terrible the situation will be. I pray for us not to be victims of this mystery in Jesus' name.

A Fake Ladder for them to Rise

A treacherous lover could ask you to let's rent an apartment and begin to pay together. But only to be sorry at the long run, complaints become his or her subjects of the day. *"Oh my business is not just moving nor flourishing any more. They haven't paid us. Nothing is happening; it looks as if everything is just turning upside-down with me lately. I just don't know what to do. Is this me Piro or Angy baby who used to help people and even given them a house to stay freely?"*

I can't imagine. With the presentation of a self pitied, you would resign to petting them with words of encouragement that all hope is not lost. You can still make it. Such are some of their tactics, just to have you spend your own as a ladder for them to rise.

Human beings, is it not this secular world or is there another world besides this? That was then, if it were even a reality at all; let alone. Meanwhile, a neighbour who seems dying to your naked eyes with all inward pretensions is secretly sending their money to construct projects or one or two things somewhere you don't even know. You will use your money to pay his or her rent and bills in order to retain the place where both of you can lay your heads. Who is the fool? Helping others is never in anyway a godly kind of foolish act. It is human beings that make it. They are usually the first to bring suggestions and also the first to brake it.

Let's be eating together, later no more contribution to shopping for the house yet feeding on the resources of other co-inhabitants. Is that fair an act to do? Due to your spirit of charity which I believe everybody has, you end up spending the whole of your money on feeding; depending on your resources anyway. He or she will still be the first to laugh at you to scorn that you have not been able to achieve anything all these years. May the good Lord of justice punish such elements that serve as agents of relegation and set back to even poverty.

Autonomous Consumption

Feeding is economically regarded by the economists as autonomous consumption. That means whether or not you are a zero income or salary earner, your stomach must demand for something—food. Someone will heartlessly obtain and drain his fellow this way and yet turned around a mocker. You are nothing but a complete devil if you are that kind of person. Look, you have done nothing but bite the finger that fed you. Only God can save you from the consequences. You thought it was smart. May God help your soul.

He or she will ironically claim to love you but fooling you and then begin to call you ignorant. While you are just busy putting something together for house rent and feeding, including bills, he or she is busy cleaning up with an elegant outfit. Sometimes, even if you have no party with those that listen to any side talk, please, do listen whenever his or her friends comes around. I bet you dear, you are definitely going to hear a word, which will make you wise up. You don't need any prophet to help you out rather they are actually going to show you a way out. You are going to gather a lot with wisdom to measure up and also to follow him or her up.

Bad people teach us a lesson sometimes. They help us with what we would take to be wise. The wise ones do not need a native doctor. A problem they say, will surely provide the victim with the corresponding solution for a way out. But in that case, you must be matured.

A Better Tomorrow

Do not resign to quarrelling with nobody; that is not the solution. The solution is either you make a separation to rent and stay on your own for peace to reign. This is because, the fact that both of you dwell together one defaulted and defrauded the other does not mean the end. There could be one or two things you must do together again in the nearest future.

And so, you can see why today must be settled amicably; the reason is nothing but for a better tomorrow. You could seldom see and greet and chat on the way or even on social media. Or even have a heart to heart talk at a quiet moment when both of you are in good mood to doing that which might likely be for a business as regard future outreach.

CHAPTER 36

Cunning Love

The Expectations of a Pretender

People ironically pretended to develop a kind of love whereby when critically analysed you discovered that they mean a different thing all together. It could just simply be considered a kind of hate in the container but love or like the contents. If you are the type that watch so very carefully, you will see that eye-service lies in their exhibitions. And such love is dangerous to rely on or else one may just fall victim as due to the expectation of the pretender.

If they tell you anything is black believe you me it might just be white or even red. Such fellows are not straight forwarded people nor are they in anyway trustworthy. They are full of dodging even their so called bosom friends. People like that are always curious eventually all about your secrete while their own is intact. Every time they feel even wiser than you do. They are the first set of people to mock at you if peradventure you fail in anything.

Their Name is Chameleon

Their name is Chameleon. If you have a friendship among that set of people, ordinarily or just to be able to beat the gravity of their opposition, be rest assured that the relationship will never last. If care is not taken, you may even give them some hidden clue about yourself to hurt you the more. The fact is that you are definitely going to realise that the motives of your relationships just can't merge.

Darkness and light can never agree: just as truth and lies can't. You could either be betrayed by them due to his interest in money in place of their heart, in love for you. If he is a boy or a man, your girlfriend is not saved even your wife if care is not taken. Forget moral conduct here as a defence to covering her up on her behalf; he can do anything to fooling you if you don't outsmart him. If she is a girlfriend or a proposal, forget it; she will definitely use you to top other boys or men and later dump you. That is to tell you that some human beings can say one thing and actually mean another. The motive of human beings can change at any time, believe you me.

Similarly, if both of you do business together and they do not cheat on you, nothing is done yet. Everything this fellow does must involve deceit. He or she is so cunning that he will even appear physically innocent on the face but inside completely dangerous, even deadly.

The tongue is so sharp and sugar that whatever he or she does wrong does not count nor even admit by the public that he is the one responsible. The tongue is so sweet that you wouldn't mind submitting your intestine to his or her public treasure. But meanwhile, he or she is looking for where to harm you. 419 is naturally done in some cases and so be wise. I tell you there are wolves in sheep clothes. Ignorantly, cunning lover is a complete mutilator and agent of relegation; try and verify you will confirm.

CHAPTER 37

Love of Pretention

Who is a Pretender?

This is an act of claiming to be what one is not in the real sense and in the real life; which could be aimed at gaining advantage from anyone for one's enrichment. It is a form of action a character displays to showing a sign of superiority. It is a whisper to tricking any victim at a particular point in time. Anybody acting like this or displaying this form of character is called a pretender.

The question is, who is a pretender? A pretender is that person who will go behind you to close your tap of blessing and yet come around to laugh with you in order to minding your reaction as to how much you can feel the pain. How it is now with you: how life is treating you is what he or she wants to see and know. A minor crash could trigger them to do such wickedness to you. A minor issue which could be settled amicably is being taken so very high that one would think that one has committed a heinous crime.

Can you imagine? It can even be taken to a coven for a retaliation. What else if not a witchcraft power in the heart of the operator as the direct tool in form of personality in the hand of Satan at a particular point in time to disrupt. If you do not activate your known and unknown connection to Satan the devil, he just can't use you; never, no never. It is only a heart full of evil that can resign to such unforgiveness carried out by you. Why would you want to destroy the source of income to your neighbour just because you got a little crash?

Hunger

The highest war that can kill even those who do not carry guns or any weapons of war to engage in the physical battle as to conclude it is the weapons that provoke war is hunger. Your intention is to completely mutilate such a targeted body of an individual intelligently by stopping his or her source of feeding. Don't you rather think you are a complete but an intelligent felony secretly working for the devil? May God forgive and deliver you.

Why? Why should you decide to switch into destroying someone's food rather than resigning to addressing the problem directly as it is and the form by which it comes? Why do you recruit other elements to assist you to execute evil, pain, flop, unemployment and even death on your targeted victims for over just a common crash? Why? Do you think man that such is evadable? No form of sin done secretly, openly, knowingly and deliberate manner of approach, seduction etc., and what you have before God under the sun will never go unpunished. That is why the scriptures says: *"The wicked will never go unpunished,"* and *"Whatsoever a man sow that shall he reap" (Prov. 11:21, Gal. 6:7-9).*

Perverting your Anointing

Why did you allow yourself to be manipulated into a complete terror against your innocent fellows? Remember you cannot manipulate God to your taste. Bear it in mind that God is not happy with you and that you have suddenly made yourself a stormy block to others by perverting your anointing.

The fact that you got that influence with which you can remote control those in authority and leadership positions does not mean you should urge them in order to help fulfilling certain evil assignments for you on innocents souls that you take for enemies just to satisfy your evil fleshly desire. And you must agree with me, there's no freedom for the wicked. It might take time but will certainly happen and that doesn't mean that you can go away with it.

As many that take the world to be personal, you do not need a prophet to define who they are to you. It is obvious by their fruit we shall know them (Matt. 7:15-20). Some riff-raff, incompetents and *"incomplete head of tuber of yams,"* I may tag them, can brag around by looking down on others when forming to show-up and appearing with swag, they are actually not but just to claim a kind of superiority before other classes of human beings and even their equals.

There's always a Payback

They can only intimidate that's all; nothing more. They lack originality in the real sense. If you watch them very closely, they are very proud with a haughty look even before everybody. Whereas, they are just like *"a butterfly that thinks itself a bird."* They are nothing but a cheat; in short, a spiritual and physical criminal who survives by the sweat of others to live their lives. Does a parasitic life pay? If at all, how is it on the long run? Does it usually augur well with the interference? There is actually nothing without a return pay-back. This is why you must desist from dubiousness and turn up a new live. Loss of focus in the highest order is for a man to live a life of another man in the whole of his or her life. What a mistake!

We have them among human races as bad life partners. If they try to lure their partners by their doings, and you disagree with them as one, you become automatically their enemy. Since you have understood immediately that the style of living is not your style, they quickly find you rigid to their kind of person because you cannot easily succumb to them nor are you flexible either to their taste. As a partner, he or she will start to abuse your person, background, family, education and social class with some deeds.

To crown it all, your standard is laughed at to scorn by them with some displayed characteristics, if you are watchful. And each time they gather spiritually and physically, your matter is their subject; it is indeed their table talk. They will so organise your hurt into having you think that their fake is original. All they do is to wholly define you negative before people with the intentions to shaming and fooling you in order to stain your reputation before even your helpers if possible. He or she can never see you as any worthy personality let alone as who will ever make it in life; and so, abuse your kind of person and your financial status. People with this type of love bird-rag all over around you always on the basis of marriage and other acquisitions.

Today is Pregnant with Tomorrow

The fact that you are married before any other close personality does not make you the alpha and omega. Life has its level with every element. And it isn't worth bragging around with. It is a totally out of babyhood by character that makes you do that. This is nature, you and I cannot define, (neither do we know) tomorrow. Look, today is pregnant but who can actually tell what tomorrow will birth? Absolutely nobody; I repeat, nobody. Anything can change in between the seconds. Furthermore, they tend to threaten you with the of number of children and marriage lovers, clothes material and financial state of their lives. Ask me, why that if nothing other than the spirit of foolishness.

Peninah did a similar case against Hannah. Little did she know that she was teaching Hannah how to talk to her God: the Maker of quality babies. As Hannah forwarded her request to God: the Maker of quality babies according to (Ps. 127:3), her case was settled. Formally regarded a barren woman, she nursed six children on her breast. Wow! What a marvellous deed of His Sovereignty! May His name be praised.

A pretentious lover won't mind underrating you even before brothers, sisters, uncles, aunties, cousins, nephews, nieces, father, mother, friends and public people around them. They may tell you they were born with a golden spoon in their mouths. Such a fellow is dangerous in the sense, he or she could pet you to where you will be killed. If he or she senses some notifications that you are about to understand him, of what he wishes to befall you negatively, and what they're up to, they will want to deceive you by saying: I am not hostile, chaos and racist towards you; feel free, I was just joking. But is it not true? It is a complete lie. Who on earth can understand the heart of a man? It is desperately wicked. The scripture says something about the heart of a man (Jer. 17:9).

A Fault Finder

Furthermore, he or she will want to exhibit some kind of control over you as fiancé or fiancée. You need to see something that your matter is always a table talk by his or her people. Every now and then you settle issues of quarrel over little things, which could be overlooked because they are fault finders. Even an ordinary discussion and phone call are just enough for a couple fight. A pretentious lover has no doubt by his or her criticisms towards your mode of dressing, manner of approach and conversation or communication and other. They will either say you are not handsome or beautiful. Your structure is so valueless before them. Even your mother tone is so embarrassing and abusive before their hearings.

However hard you may try to launch deep into the waters in order to harvest so many fishes; and if possible leaving no single finger-lane behind in the body of the waters for his or her sake, your efforts still remain very primitive before their naked eyes. By taking just a stroll, window-shopping, going to church at the same time, in accompanying someone to a party, just to honour the invitation with a recommendation of a proper identification, as a girlfriend or boyfriend, fiancé or fiancée or even as couples due to wrong choices, you are not just worthy to be associated.

Free Entrance & Exit

Do you know why? You are not part of their priority. He or she prefers that no one knows that you both have anything in common. The answer is not far fetched that he or she has the intension to sneak in and sneak out in the relationship with you, if you were to view their motive. Take a close look at your spurn after both of your dates. Behold! It is like HIV positively infected to him or her; forgotten that a true love can heal. Even if a true love can truly heal, yet a kiss is an abomination to whom you tend to date or love, why? To him or her, your mouth smells badly whereas nothing like that. And the side you sleep on bed is stained. Such a fellow is a dictator. Personally, they are demonic and the spirit wants free entrance and free exit with a dramatic pay part unknowingly to the date.

Whenever he or she hungers and tastes to play that is only when both of you would want to. He or she is so very bold to demonstrate having an affair with additional fellows beside you by his actions. Such a one always sees others out there as superiors to you before their eyes. Whenever you are together he or she is a very quiet person but when he gives you a bent, my friend you are finished. This is somebody you relate every one of your secretes and future plans. O!

With this you can imagine if you co-inhabit with a non confiding fellow in an amulet, every villager must be aware of every gari you soak to bed in the previous day. Everything is pressed and aired. Whatever you do is disgustful and assorting to him or her. You are only seen by them as a load carrier, on the basis of payment of house rent and bills, buying of children school materials (that is if you are already married); that also includes shouldering the three families responsibilities all alone besides the law of your coming together from two different families as one is not adhered to. In his or her agenda, like introducing someone before others, you are not just in her gender. You find out you do not just look like someone before him or her believe me.

Personal Aggrandisement

For a personal aggrandisement, he or she has so many phone numbers she calls; some are fake while others are real. A serious date in courtship will never do that. How long will he or she do that. I don't want to believe it is money hawking. One could make the world population for a customer yet not being satisfied. Second life has rubbished many things and a lot of opportunities. Oh! You can say that again.

Do you know how many beautiful single ladies some unfaithful guys have relinquished. Do you also know how many handsome single good guys and many promiscuous fake ladies have equally relinquished a lot. Many today are crying, saying: *"Truly the world is the world and humans are humans."* One cannot eat glory. Only the Lord God can actually tell what glory is to Him. May the good God deliver someone.

Disgustfully, oh the majority are boyfriends, girlfriends, even spiritual wives and husbands to some of their same bloods, even their relatives and as such, yours to them, do not count. Can you imagine dragging your fiancé, fiancée, wife or husband indirectly with the same blood due to some notice of rigidity? Their indignation and insubordination will tell you what they are up to; that's if you are vigilant. I tell you what, they are so inquisitive who has been able to make it in your family. To you as the wise type, when things happen like that so well, it is calling for a check-up before it gets out of hand if even such a relationship will amount to marriage.

The solution is, one, it is either you call off the dating or you do some amendments before making any further step. A pretentious single lady will say, you do not know the usefulness of a woman or a lady. Your love with her is always regulated by the people and interferers of love from time to time. To them, it is usually the order of your days. Sometimes, if you got no option, what do you do? You get to bear it. The saying goes thus: *"What one cannot avoid at least one has to endure it."*

Sycophancy

Do you know what? You are just in sycophancy in your relationship with them, which is an act of sheepishness. Since you were not being regarded before, so, every little offence you commit, you must beg or keep hearing the people egging her to quit the relationship with you. Try at the initial stage of every relationship to know the position you are in his or her mind before even it matures else be prepared to cry at the last. May that not be your portion in Jesus mighty name. Stay blessed.

A Loveless Bargain

In most cases, people only concentrate on what brought them together with some other persons; without having any feeling for them on the basis of human phenomenon. If your bargain with someone has nothing to do with love, what use is it? Whether in any profession, careers, organisation, religion, status etc. you have anything in common it is for love. If you must employ any worker it is out of love. If you must dwell together, it is love. If you must study together, it is love. If you must travel together, it is love. If you must dine and wine together, it is still love; okay.

Pretension has Different Dimensions

You see, pretension has different dimensions. As a rational being, I cannot just speedily draw a conclusion over any case related to pretension. Why? Well, the truth is not far fetched in the sense, the fact that the person in question decides to come up this way, must never be any yardstick measure to castigating him. There must be a reason behind it. And so, without hearing the details, one would assume the fellow is the bad type. To me, I completely disagree to that opinion because I don't know what that fellow is concealing up or what has been his previous curriculum. It's not actually good to be judgemental. Let's examine this illustration.

Luke once proposed to a single girl for a future life partner. In short, he believed quite well that they will both marry in the nearest future. To his understanding with all confidence as a typical believer, he took to the law: marry before sex. This he strove to maintain. So, in an attempt to maintaining the law and order of the Sovereign Lord, the young Luke was abused with his genuine love. Do you know what? The guy did not know that the very girl in question was in a secret relationship with another guy; until she became pregnant, it never occurred to his knowledge that such would happen because he doesn't know how to cheat on anybody.

The Disappointment of Betrayal

When she was exposed, Luke was badly disappointed. Whenever he ruminates over the *"diamond he actually placed on the swine,"* he became so much bitter and angry with a vow never to disclose all his secretes to any of the opposite sex in any relationship, until they are both married.

Having quit the first promiscuous girl he used to have as he got another one with God so kind, this second blended to his taste by obeying his instruction and order. Even though, he later got it right, it took him pain throughout the whole processes. It became like a scar of a hero in his memory.

Back to the crux. Do you now crucify Luke for his action he took throughout, just to correct errors and mistakes in the past which caused him pain? If you leave a crime person to go free he or she may take it as a culture. But we thank the Lord that no sin will ever receive its due punishment. And not all histories are pleasant, certainly are so provocative. Remember she broke his heart almost to the point of committing suicide or even death.

Innocents

Then, what are we talking about? In a nutshell, this we must know is a complete warning for us to take caution mostly those of us who are still singles and the young generation who are also innocent about life. The tale so far caused someone with pain which we just narrated. The reason why history, it is for a future correction but has to be limited in order to avoid disaster. Most importantly, it is because we all do make mistakes of choices as a result of lack of understanding. Note, there are hidden agendas of God's creation. However, the proportion that the Lord God allotted to us for our understanding must be striven to understand for our own good.

That which we must know does induce pain with anyone in question. Issues about life which cuts across this basic fact in particular pass to us humans with rigorous training. My advice is that, if one does not want to continue to cry due to broken relationships, one shouldn't be too swift to draw conclusion in any relationship without juxtaposing over the past mistakes and experiences which were humanly drastic to the core.

Honestly, there are really initiators or even instigators; when it comes to love with pretension. I was to dam this issue as a subject but when I came to my senses, I then realised it is actually worth discussing in other to derive elements of senses. Equivocally, I feel I should make this officially clear to us that in any case, we must never remain in the category of ignorant else we relinquish much advantage as far as our positive expectations are concerned.

CHAPTER 38

Love of Food

Embracing the Good Life

You and I love food. We eat food. We go for entertainment, we love entertainment and embrace entertainment where we go and take some merriment: dine and wine, flex and take some refreshment even catch fun together. We buy clothes and wear them in order to look good in our outfit. We all strive to live the best of life to the fullest. You and I have a background or family, each of which only you can define your own better. Only you can tell whether you once suffered malnutrition or even hailed from a home where three square-meals daily were a problem or not.

We were not the ones that created food. At a time, it is discovered harmless and good for a consumption. But it was confirmed worthy of consumption that is why we feed on the concerned types of food each time we are hungry. Food is a part of human culture in the sense the one you are familiar with will actually determine what you eat at a particular point in time; provided it is harmless. On social media today you can guess relatively close to, if not accurately, a particular set of people some persons are by race because food has so much to define about them with culture.

What is your Business?

Food is defined as anything, substance, liquid and gas that man and animal (even plants), consume in order to sustain life. But I heard you say, *"I eat too much."* And that I am gluttonous you said. What is your business if I eat the food of the entire world? If I made myself voracious what is your business? If I use my whole salaries for enjoyment what is your business? If I flex all days what is your business? If I go from party to party, what is your business? What is your business if I only come out once in a gloom moon?

That is, if what I have is not almost finished I usually do not come out to look for more; otherwise, I am always indoors 24 hours a day, day in and day out, what is your business? Are you my next of kin? My consumption is my own benefit; whether or not I have heaven and earth. If really the true love is there you would call me to order to sort it out peacefully rather than making an uproar to create awareness by it to a third party.

If I am stupid can't you call me to order if you really love me? If I am foolish can't you call me to order for good?

A rational person will always consider the reaction of the audience before any oral or verbal kind of action for good because of future dealings with each other.

Honestly speaking, we all know that one of the basic necessities of life is food. If one must live, one needs food. But some people have over loved food that breeze cannot just blow across their stomachs. It gives energy anyway but when it over-consumed, you get constipation. Nutrients derived from food intake nourish you and make you look fresh and healthy.

Good Nourishment

It is true that food helps your immune system to fight disease in the body. Adequate feeding regularly on good food helps to minimise the rate at which one risks falling sick and thereby frequent the hospital for check-ups and treatment. It busts your immune system. Whatever such a fellow is doing, there is always a full concentration; with active and retentive memory. Diversification of thought is of a minimum rate with who feeds well on good food.

Children who receive and enjoy adequate feeding grow rapidly. It assists hormones for growth and that quickens the sizes and lengths of the body structure, besides traits from the parents. They are likely to do well in schools far better than the under nourished. Anybody who feeds well does not know nothing about lippy except by witchcraft. Such a person is very humbled and polite. They usually do not grow angry so easily just like that. One other great advantage of the love of food is that it boosts much interest in reproduction. Take a look at the background of any prolific woman, you will find out that it wasn't possible if not for adequate care which was made available with her. A well taken care of woman can birth a village, trust me.

Food Habits

If you form a particular habit for food, enemy will use it against you as an attack if care is not taken. And if it is on a particular kind of food, you may likely be poisoned by it. Bewitchment is of different kinds. May the good God deliver us. For example, 11:30—13:00 in some countries is usually the period eventually every worker goes to eat during break hour. If you see the road this time around, everywhere is rounding.

Some of the civil servants whose houses are very close to their various working places and more also those who are personally mobile will prefer to go eat at home and if possible even take their sister. This has caused accident several times by reckless drivers. As far back 2002 on one faithful afternoon, between 12:00 in the mid-afternoon— 12:30 p.m. or thereabout, a student was just crossing through zebra cross/across the road lanes, there was also this driver who also was coming at the spot in a hurry to go home on break just to do the usual thing or normal rout, unfortunately he hit at this student up so very high and landed him on the ground.

This student was left to rest for a couple of minutes according to the law enforcement agents who came at the spot, if otherwise he was touched he would die and that is the end they instructed. Every of his fellow student was crying at aloof and at the scene. Meanwhile, the law says, if you hit somebody on a zebra crossing, your driving licence will be confiscated until further notice.

It was still this same style of unanimous eating time that some menaces were allegedly reported used against some nations in the world as a medium for an invasion or attack in the past histories. It is a period used as unaware by the enemies to invade the territory of their targeted victims for an attack. It is realised therefore that too much of everything is bad. And so, caution yourselves and you must know when you are to stop or rather limit in anything you are doing to avoid law of diminishing return, which may likely be unpleasant to receive by you. Help yourself before even you are helped by any good Samaritan.

CHAPTER 39

Love of Profession

Paid Occupation

Profession is a paid occupation especially the one that involves prolonged training and a formal qualification. It could as well be defined as the career choice or a call. There is no born element who does not like and delight in whatever he/she does which gives him most especially what he needs to be sustained in life. There are so many professions like: all kinds of jobs, and even criminal activities. An assassin is a profession undertaken by some personalities, just like every other element like you and I who will undertake a legal job to survive the only thing is that, theirs is against the law .

As students like school because at nearest in future, it will definitely be like a torrent after a long drought, which must supersede every form of dry-season in his or her life. What you like too much is a problem. I think average should be better off.

Education

Actually, education is the key to success. The interest in it is very important and high. And that propels the motivation to embark on it, which is so solid in foundation with all kinds of diversifications. In it, you have different kind of studies which determine your outcome and profession known as the "scopes". People do not just like a particular profession or job for liking sake. In most cases, they like it because of what it will yield them.

For example, if you like to study accounting in school, it means, you know that at the end of the whole process, you are going to work in the bank and earn fine. The money involved there is what boosts the moral of those that are concerned. Apart from money motive, some professions attract dignity to those that undertake them. No one that doesn't like to be famous. A guy was interviewed some time ago about what purposed him to be a GNLD distributor? He said he wanted to be famous.

Strictly speaking, some jobs are less strenuous while others are tedious. Even a common illiterate farmer hates a hackuliar job to do for a living. Even if it is possible and there where away for him to avert his undertaking for another with less stressful method, he would do just that. The law breakers or the recalcitrance who live a parasitic lives do like criminal act because it is their profession which serves as their sources of dependable income for survival.

If you're not Informed you're Deformed

There are criminals by gun, biro, tongue and cheating, according to categories and are deeply rooted from spiritual and physical realms as recruited criminals from the dark world as their foundational background. Of all, Jehovah is the answer anyway; because if you escape the physical there is every tendency that you might likely be a victim to the spiritual. If you are not informed you are deformed. But only God can assure you of adequate security and a safe landing of it all.

Ministry Profile

Doctor Agene Justice Onotiemoria (A.J.O.) hails from Uwessan Ibhiolulu, Irrua Essan Central Local Government of Edo State Nigeria. He had his primary education in Uwessan Ibhiolulu, Irrua, his post primary education in Ujabhole Grammar School, Ujabhole, Irrua and Agba Grammar School, Uromi, all in Edo State. A degree holder in Theology from LifeStyle International Christian University, Firenze Italy.

The author is humility personified, kind hearted, soft spoken and cool-headed gentleman to the core. A seasoned writer, a preacher and a pioneer of righteousness. An ordained worker of God's Vineyard as a financial secretary, an usher, a gospel musician, a member of the choir, youth speaker and a deacon. He was formerly a distributor to G.N.L.D. (an Italian company), a civil servant to Bendel Construction Company Limited (B.C.C.L.) Nigeria, and a furniture maker. He is married with a wife and children.

To Contact the Author

Please email:

Agene Justice Onotiemoria
Email: littlejustice508@gmail.com

*Please include your prayer requests
and comments when you write.*

Other Books

Love
(Love Distinguished - Series One)

This is a book about Love, in both its negative and positive lights, such as: the love of parents and family, the love of riches and materialism, including the love of patriotism and even unemployment. We will even discuss inappropriate love, such as incest and the use of rituals and so forth.

ISBN: 978-1-909132-28-3, Pages: 244, Format: Paperback, Published: 2023
Also available in eBook format!

The Heart of Love
(Love Distinguished - Series Three)

The Heart of Love has to be received by the Love of Truth; it is a positive foundational footing for any house that wishes to stand. It is also known as justice that builds a nation. The bible says: The righteous are as bold as lions (Proverbs 28:1).

ISBN: 978-1-909132-31-3, Pages: 255, Format: Paperback, Published: 2023
Also available in eBook format!

**Sweet Bitter Love
(Love Distinguished - Series Four)**

Dr. Justice again has put together stimulating truth, saying that you cannot see someone and quickly conclude that they are your bosom friends. In other words, don't be too fast to put your trust or love in those that might turn out to be bitter or sweet.

ISBN: 978-1-909132-83-2, Pages: 246,
Format: Paperback, Published: 2023
Also available in eBook format!

**Stolen Love
(Love Distinguished - Series Five)**

In this last book of this series, the writer declares that whoever one may be, whatever they do, no matter their race, background, education, class, height, structure, beauty, handsome, rich, poor, barren, married or single or otherwise, they must not allow true love to be distorted or stolen. Remember, all must stand before Him.

ISBN: 978-1-909132-84-9, Pages: 237,
Format: Paperback, Published: 2023
Also available in eBook format!

TONY OSCAR
Musical Artist
LOOK ME UP ON YOUTUBE
@tonyoscar

All Books Available

at

APMI PUBLICATIONS

Email: publications@alanpateman.com
*Also Available from Amazon.com
and other retail outlets.*